The Time-Out
Traveller

Let us endeavor so to live that when we come to die even the undertaker will be sorry.

(Mark Twain, *The Tragedy of Pudd'nhead Wilson and The Comedy those Extraordinary Twins*)

The Time-Out Traveller

Darryl Sailor

First published in the United Kingdom in 2011 by
Darryl Sailor

Copyright © Darryl Sailor 2011

All photography by Darryl Sailor

All rights reserved. No part of this publication may be reproduced or transmitted in any form or by any means, electronic or mechanical including photocopying, recording or any information storage or retrieval system, without prior permission in writing from the publishers.

ISBN 978-0-9567488-0-5

Book production by
The Choir Press

For Mum

Contents

Introduction	1
China	15
New Zealand	33
Australia	57
India	81
Southern Africa	
Mozambique	101
South Africa	107
Namibia	114
Botswana	120
Zimbabwe	125
South America	
Peru	131
Ecuador	137
Argentina	148
(and a little bit of) Chile	164
(and back to) Argentina	168
Brazil	176
North America	
United States of America	195
(and a little bit of) Canada	227

Japan	237
Epilogue	251
About the Author	253

Introduction

I've just turned forty, got married and quit my job.

I'll say that again for you to read a little more slowly.

I've just turned forty,

got married and

quit my job.

And one last time to make sure it sinks in as it took me a very long time (forty years to be precise) to get myself into this delightful position.

I've just turned forty, got married and quit my job!!!

Wow, even by my own personal standards this is shaping up to be a big year.

Now, I couldn't do much about the former but the latter were obviously choices. That wonderful process afforded to us by nature and capitalism. And until you make the choices you are of course not sure they're the right ones. But as the famous saying goes (paraphrased), regret is for the things you didn't do.

Well, I can tell you so far so good on the marriage front. We'll see how the job quitting goes in the year to come.

Aha, I hear you say. This man is obviously having a mid-life crisis. Now, I've thought about this for a long time, as I do with most important decisions, and I can with some conviction tell you I'm not. Anyway, I had one of those when I was thirty-four. I know that now, but didn't at the time, as it's only with hindsight you can spot the symptoms, rash decisions and resultant consequences. But I digress.

I know you don't believe me this early on in the story though so we'll talk a little more on the point.

Well, I have to concede that turning forty is classic mid-life crisis territory. I've just become a cliché and stereo-typical male all in one day. So, I've obviously ditched the first wife, married a younger model and bought a sports car, right? I've also obviously taken a better job which I was able to get by virtue of my receding hairline, expanding waistline and cynical exterior honed from years of corporate life.

No, no and thrice no.

This is my first marriage, and has been well worth the wait. The missus is my long-term partner, the most special lady in the world to me and deserves the best I can give her and then some. It really wasn't a hard decision in the end.

I've had sports cars for years, have petrol running through my veins and traffic police frequently running through my chequebook. But the cars have just been sold.

Until the start of this year I was the regional director

of a multimillion dollar business. I was good at it too. I know this as they kept me for a decade, paid me well, gave me bonuses and were unhappy to see me leave. I didn't leave to take a new job.

My wife would describe me as youthful, optimistic, full of energy and rather handsome. She's obviously biased though. Oh yes, my hair is stubbornly remaining on my head and the belly is in check (albeit I'm not going to be challenging Mr Pitt to a six-pack contest anytime soon).

So why quit working?

Obviously you need money to not work. Yep, the bills that came in during your working life keep coming in when you're not working. A bit of an obvious statement I know but worth mentioning as we don't plan on selling our house and very much want to return to something resembling our home life at some point in the future.

My wife doesn't come from a rich family and neither do I so there's no inheritance. Neither of us has won the lottery either; or robbed a bank. In fact we were both born with a plastic rather than a silver spoon in our mouths and only have what we've been able to toil for.

It works out though that this is enough to take a sabbatical, to coin the current in-vogue phrase. So that's exactly what we're doing.

I'll get to the family, friends and colleagues' reaction to our plans in a while but suffice to say the majority of people concluded they lovingly hate us for doing what they wish they had themselves done. Who knows, we may well have inspired a few to make the leap in the months and years to come. I do hope so.

There are many things to do with the life you're

given and trying out a few of them for more than a weekend or the period of your annual leave shouldn't only be a goal we all aim for but something we actually do when the opportunity presents itself. Believe me there are a hundred and one reasons you'll come up with to convince yourself you can't do it. I know, I've been coming up with them for years. Ultimately, there's only one reason you'll do it – because you really want to. Personally, I'd also hate to reach retirement and look back on a missed opportunity that I really should have taken and will forever be ruing.

So, what to do with the time now I've freed it up?

My job took me all over the world, literally. I would generally be away from home for six months of the year in one-, two- or three-week trips and sometimes for much longer periods. This resulted in a lot of air miles and hotel points (very handy for annual holidays) but not enough time with loved ones. So travelling for a year is probably a silly thing to do. Better to stay home, relax, take up a new sport or hobby. Maybe discover our spirituality, do some charity work or learn a new skill. People keep mentioning babies too.

Hell no. That lot can wait. We're off on a round the world trip for a whole year. Yep, that promise a lot of people keep telling themselves they're going to make happen. Sometimes you just have to put up or shut up. We couldn't be happier putting rather than shutting.

We both have a deep love of travelling you see. No amount of business travel will satiate that as you generally only get to see the inside of a taxi, hotel, office and airport and are very rarely with someone you want to be travelling with. The work tends to get in the way too.

We're both educated people but obtained those

educations through working and studying at the same time. No twentysomething pre- or post-university gap year to have soaked up the wanderlust in years gone by.

Through holidaying or work I've been to the four corners of the earth, as the saying goes, plus seventy-odd countries beside. Seems there are over two hundred countries these days though so still plenty to work with. Going to the same place again in a few cases would also be very nice. Reacquainting one's self with past locations that were memorable cannot be a bad thing.

Right, I think that just about brings you up to speed with how I find myself at this point. Having done so, I now need to make an addition to the opening sentence.

I've just turned forty, got married, quit my job and am about to go on a one-year around the world trip!

Okay. So this needs some planning then, but how hard can that be? My secretary can get my business trips booked the same day and holidays historically only take a few days to put together so I'd imagine this time next week it'll all be sorted. Let's add some contingency to that and say two weeks. You can see my business training and optimistic nature coming to the fore I'm sure.

First things first, let's decide where we're going to go. We figured, let's both come up with a separate list of countries and places/sights, compare notes and log down those we both want to go to. We'll then negotiate over the rest taking into account available time, how well that location fits into the overall plan, accessibility, cost and places that can be more easily saved for a separate future excursion.

Cue a nice bottle of red, an atlas and the internet.

Two weeks later and we've just about finished deciding where we've going, and we're still talking. I think a time revision of the planning stage is in order and I think I need to buy my wife a present.

In fact, when all was said and done it took us the best part of five months to organize. And there will be sections of the trip that we'll organize as we go on top of what's been organized to get us going. Good job we actually started organizing before I quit my job.

Getting on a plane on day one and returning only on day three hundred and sixty-five is harder than it sounds.

Yes, I know we could have got a third party to organize it, but where's the fun in that? Sure, if you're on a few weeks away and hassled with work for the rest of the year it makes sense but we're not and I really think the organizing is an essential part of the experience. Having gone through the trip-planning process ourselves now, which has ultimately been a knowledgeable and enjoyable exercise (albeit interspersed with hair-pulling frustration) we're in much better shape for the actual trip. We now know the full details almost by heart. We also have spoken on the phone with the proprietors of hotels, lodges and guest houses across the globe and have a human element to look forward to when we arrive and get to meet the people who've helped us arrange accommodation and excursions.

I guess we could have booked a few flights and then just headed off and organized things as we went. Having gone through the process of organizing a large portion of the adventure in advance though it's now obvious to me that such a laissez-faire approach to the trip would have resulted in massive frustration, undue stress and probably missed experiences as it's certain a lot of what we want to see and do would have been fully booked, out of season or have no connecting flight from the point on the globe we hadn't planned to be at.

Now, I think it's also worth pointing out at this time that whilst we plan on seeing a lot, it's not the intention to be racing around the globe Phileas Fogg style to 'see it all'. We want to remember the trip, the people, the places and the experiences and have as such lopped off great chunks of must-see places to preserve this goal. We've hopefully got another thirty years or more thereafter to spend time exploring the bits we didn't go to on this trip anyway.

So with the places set out and agreed we turned our attention to the accommodation.

As I mentioned at the beginning, I'm forty. My wife is in her thirties and generally somewhere clean and indoors is preferred of an evening. I remember clearly being informed by my better half that she'll put up with a lot on this trip but digging a hole and shitting in it is a non-starter. There must be somewhere for a shower and the toilet must have a door on it. I do love her. This has led to several friends referring to our trip as 'champagne back-packing'.

As you can imagine we've had rather a few discussions on the whole enterprise.

We had one friend who quite earnestly and in all seriousness asked why we were going away for a year to see all these places when we could sit at home of an evening with a glass of wine and watch them on TV.

Another friend asked if I thought we'd still be married when we returned as a year is a long time to be with the missus without a break. He's single by the way.

Yet others seemed to think giving up such a good career was a bad move. Is a year off really giving up a career though? I think not.

Generally, people have been wishing they had done the same thing at our time in life. You have sufficient experience, knowledge, energy and cash to make the very best of it. You don't yet have kids and your enthusiasm for life and continuing new experience is still intact. Why would you not?

When I think back at the process I went through to make the big decision to quit working for a while, you do in fact have all these thoughts and more over rather a long time (with the possible exception of sitting at home and watching it on TV). We do appear to be in rather a small minority of people making such a decision though from what I can gather. To give up chasing the next incremental job title, car model upgrade or other materialistic experience doesn't seem such a sacrifice to make having made the decision, but before you make it, it appears to be a rather difficult mistress to leave.

So, we're over the hump as they say and it'll all be plain sailing from here on to coin another phrase and shoehorn rather too many metaphors into one sentence.

Well yes, and no.

Yes, the hard decision is made and the world hasn't stopped spinning and we haven't reverted to cave dwelling and charitable handouts. No, there's an awful lot to do. Well splendid I say.

Time to get the itinerary populated.

This is where the real work comes in. Having a computer, the internet and a partner who can fly around cyberspace with the ease of an eighteen-year-old computer hacker is a must. Check, check and check.

Whilst I've been in charge of the trip's overview and making sure we're going to be going to the right places, using various modes of transport in the chosen countries etc., my wife's skills at finding suitable travel agencies, flights and accommodation are now in need.

After a few days staring at the computer we're thinking we also need to buy a few more travel guides and enlist the help of friends. Internet search engines are a very good place to start but sometimes you just wish there were fewer options to choose from and that those options were all of an ilk that suited your intended itinerary. Good job my wife has the patience of a saint when it comes to research.

We have benefited from having an international network of close friends who, like us, travel and hence have ideas of how to go about certain parts of the trip. This proved very helpful in making final decisions on certain travel ideas.

We're also visiting a few countries where a friend or two live. These sectors we're finding easy to organize as the local knowledge is priceless and said friends are joining us on parts of the trip to boot. This has the added benefit of giving us an outlet that may help avoid the impending divorce at least one of our friends feels we're rushing headlong into.

Other countries and regions where English or Mandarin are not the chosen language are proving a little harder as neither of us can speak the lingo but it's turning out to be fun trying (particularly with the help of free online translator tools: a surefire way of ensuring you can unwittingly insult anyone on the globe in thirty different languages).

So you probably want to know where we're going, right?

Okay, here's the short version.

First leg is China. We're going to travel from Beijing to Lhasa via Xian and Chengdu.

Then it's a tour of North and South New Zealand followed by a tour of Australia and Tasmania.

A quick hop up to India to travel across from Kolkata (formerly Calcutta) to Mumbai (formerly Bombay) and then we're off to Southern Africa.

Mozambique to South Africa to Namibia to Botswana to Zimbabwe.

Next we'll be touring a large chunk of South America and heading all the way down to the 'bottom of the world': Tierra del Fuego.

Heading north we'll cross the USA and parts of Canada and finish the trip in Japan before heading home to Singapore.

What was that about NOT doing a Phileas Fogg? I hear you say!

Okay, it may not be for the faint hearted but it's really not that rushed when you break it down.

We've figured out that we'll take a few driving tours that we both find relaxing. This is a great way to see a country. You can travel at your own pace, avoid the crowds and take the road less travelled as you see fit. We're also staying in each country/region for no less than three weeks and in most cases a month or more. Our past trips to North America, South America, Oceania, Africa, the Middle East and Asia also mean large chunks of the globe can be missed on this trip, having previously experienced them.

Being British, and hence sort of European, and the missus having toured big parts of the continent years ago we felt Europe could be lopped off the list too. It's earmarked for one or more future holidays though as the multitude of cultures, incredible art and architecture, not to mention some of the geography and of course the food needs experiencing again and again.

Living in South East Asia for the last decade, and my wife being Singaporean, means most of that region has been explored by both of us either together or independently. We'll be going back to live in Singapore after the trip too so it's on our doorstep for the future. And what an incredible doorstep that is. With Angkor Wat – Cambodia; Halong Bay – Vietnam, Bagan – Myanmar; the islands and beaches of Thailand; Borobodur – Indonesia; Mount Kinabalu – Malaysia, and a hundred other sights, places, cultures and culinary experiences there's a whole year or more just in this one corner of the world.

Did I forget to mention that the sun's shining for most days of the year too?

That just leaves the Arctic and Antarctic polar regions plus Russia as places we'd have liked to go to but have decided not to. Cost and time are a big factor with either polar region; the south in particular is extremely expensive to reach and very time consuming as you need to float there. The latter reason alone takes it out of contention as it would have meant sacrificing too many of the other destinations we both really wanted to experience. We're compensating by going to all four of the world's most southerly land masses: Tierra del Fuego, Cape Horn, Tasmania and New Zealand's South Island. There's bound to be some snow in one of them and most have penguins, whales and sea lions too. The northern polar region of course has polar bears. Will be a pity to miss them but there's always next year.

And after thinking about Russia we came to the conclusion that it was only really St Petersburg and Moscow we wanted to go to. It would be a very big detour from the chosen itinerary we settled on to go there just for that. Plus it seems Mother Russia isn't too keen on giving out visas months in advance of visiting and getting one when you're on the road is filed under 'extremely difficult'. So off the list it came.

Now, in truth there were several other countries we'd have loved to squeeze in but as I said earlier we're trying to avoid squeezing so after wringing our hands for a while we took the decision and made the cut.

So there you have it.

Time to pack.

China

China

Hutongs and the Bellyman

I've been to Beijing before, but it's changed quite rapidly since my first trip in 2002.

China has become more wealthy and with it a lot of shiny new buildings have popped up to house the population, the arts, the state TV channels and the visiting world.

The Olympics in 2008 saw a push to 'green' the city and improve the air quality. This included the planting of a million trees and the relocation of factories out of town. It also saw programmes to spruce up the locals' social skills and wholescale painting of the relics from a bygone empire to spruce up the tourist trail.

Millions of bicycles have been replaced with millions of cars. Not sure the locals have taken what would pass as a rigorous driving test to pilot those cars though as they never seem to stop, except at red lights, and everyone appears to have the right of way. This includes those walking or pedalling who appear to have a wanton abandon to maintaining their lives. There's a distinct feeling as a bystander that everyone is 'using the force' Jedi style as what you think is an imminent T-boning just seems to pass without incident time and again. Just as in decades past when bicycles ruled supreme on Beijing's streets it seems to sort of work but I'm not convinced enough to get behind the wheel on this trip and resolve to remain a passenger.

A year later, after the Olympics have gone, the trees are still standing but I guess a few million more are needed as the pollution over the city is omnipresent and spoiling the view somewhat. Victorian era industrial revolution smog is what I'm describing here. Twenty-four hours and your throat's raspy and your eyes are sore. Your camera is also annoyed as it can't see anything.

All's not bad though and a few days in the capital were rather enjoyable. With such wonderful empire relics on show as the Forbidden City, Temple of Heaven, the Great Wall, the Summer Palace and many more it would be hard not to be impressed.

It all started with being picked up at the airport in a London taxi cab. Yep, that very English of transports has made its way over to the Middle Kingdom. Seems it's also a bit of an odd sight to the locals as you'd have got less reaction from onlookers if you were in a Ferrari.

The driver was hilarious too. Well that's what my wife told me as he only told jokes in Mandarin. He also knew his highways from his streets and hutongs as he found the place we'd booked to stay in with ease. You see, we'd decided not to stay in a standard hotel. We were going to get a taste of old Beijing and stay in a converted courtyard house in the hutongs.

The word literally translates as 'alley'. Rather narrow alleys too as the cabbie found out when he drove in and we couldn't open the doors as they were wedged up against a wall on each side. A girl in pyjamas on a bicycle thought this amusing until she realized she couldn't get by. Some more of the locals then joined the scene including a woman in a nightie and a builder in wellington boots brushing his teeth. By this time though we'd reversed enough to open one back door and dragged our bags out, leaving the cabbie to agonize over how to reverse one hundred metres down an alley with his wing mirrors virtually scrapping the walls on both sides. This was our first encounter with the local residents and was to become the start of many an encounter with a Beijing the government probably doesn't want you to see let alone partake of.

You see, the hutongs surround the Forbidden City. This means they occupy some of Beijing's best land as they are right in the heart of the city. But no rich people live here that we've noticed. They're largely occupied by working class families at the top end and those hovering around peasantry at the bottom end. As with council housing in the UK and the projects in the US, a certain amount of uneducated behaviour can hence be expected. For example, it didn't take long for us to realize that the social programme to get rid of spitting hasn't reached this deep into society. Even the women do it and I was somewhat startled to hear a great loogie being hocked behind me and on turning around, as much out of curiosity as making sure I was out of firing range, to see a little old lady letting loose a full fat bullet.

The people here are what would euphemistically be called colourful I'd say. Not overly welcoming, say like an American who's invited you out for a drink after a thirty-second chat in an elevator, but on the pleasant side of 'I don't really want to talk to you but you're white and standing in my way so I'll smile, look you up and down and say hello'. They also don't seem to really care that their social foibles and clothes can often be unfit for public consumption. Walking around in your underwear washing your face with a flannel is best left to the bathroom I find. They do seem to have an ability to make such things endearing though.

By far the most interesting character in this real life street theatre was the Beijing Bellyman. I've just made that name up but it may yet become a new demographic for the marketeers out there. The summer heat no doubt accounts for the Bellyman's attire but nonetheless it's a look I've yet to see anywhere outside of China.

An undervest hitched up over a rotund middle-aged beer belly to just below nipple height is set off with boxer shorts, sports socks and loafers. After seeing a couple in quick succession I was attuned and could spot them all over the city. Yes, this look had successfully migrated out of the hutongs. There were even upmarket ones with branded polo shirts and American-style checked shorts (you know, the ones you see on men of a certain age and golfers) but the sports socks and loafers seemed to be a constant. Nicely dressed wives and girlfriends accompanied the upmarket Bellyman and bizarrely didn't seem to mind. Don't judge a book by its cover, or poor eyesight?

I managed to get a few photos without being spotted. Well, you need a few piccies to show friends the oddities of the world, don't you? They didn't seem to really care that a 'long nose' was snapping them anyway, probably because they generally showed no sign of feeling conspicuous even though they were sporting a look that offers no redeeming features except humour for the onlooker.

I fear such delightful eccentricity may have its days numbered in the hutongs though. The rich want a piece of the action (the real estate, not the Bellyman) and the hutongs are changing. From what I can gather from speaking to the owner of our residence and a few taxi drivers, the poor have occupied the hutongs since the cultural revolution and a lot of them prefer the life to living in high rise condominiums away from the ancient heart of the city. Yet others have been there for generations longer.

The elite are taking over though and either demolishing the areas, building new structures and relocating the residents, or buying and restoring them to their former glory from when bound feet and silk robes were in fashion.

It'll be a pity when the shoddy buildings and characterful residents have been replaced. I doubt the replacements will provide anything equal to the experience that we've spent the last few days enjoying. And I tell you what, Beijing will be the poorer for it.

Methinks this 'style' won't be picked up by the major fashion houses anytime soon!

Terracotta empires, pandas and teahouses

The world is now fairly rapidly waking up to the need for a replacement to gasoline for vehicles and some alternative fuels are starting to make headway into the market in certain parts of the world. Seems China isn't to be left out on this one.

Having left the current capital and moved to the original Qin capital of Xi'an we've noticed that some cars and almost all the motorbikes have very quiet engines. This is the city that was home to the first emperor of the united Qin empire or 'China'. It's the home of the Terracotta Warriors. A must-see attraction which I believe everyone has heard of so I won't bore you with details of how lifelike they are and every one is different. But they are, and you should definitely go to see them if you're in this region.

Now where was I? Oh yes, silent cars and motorbikes. After nearly having a heart attack from one creeping up on me without a sound I realized they're electric. Nothing new there I hear you say. A lot of countries have a few electric vehicles these days. My point though is that ALL of the motorbikes were electric. This I wasn't expecting in a country that went straight from the fields to modern glass and steel skyscrapers in a generation. But that night, quite by chance, we were treated to a first-hand experience with one of China's electric road warriors.

We had a very poor French meal in a restaurant with a stunning view of Xi'an's ancient bell tower. The French chef, who unaccountably finished working at 6pm and left the local Chinese cooks to feed the guests, unfortunately wasn't available to receive our colourful suggestions on how to improve. After a few weeks of

Chinese food we'd rashly decided to try something different. What's that old saying about repenting at leisure?

We had rather a lot of alcohol to try and erase the experience and then spent thirty minutes failing to hail a cab to take us home. What did pop up though was a young man on a three-wheeled trishaw. It was an electric one and the next twenty minutes was about to become a hoot.

Having haggled a price we hopped in behind the driver, who turned out to be one of Xi'an's sixty thousand Muslims, and without a sound sped off down the road. The acceleration on this thing was, well, electric. With tyres and handlebars from a bicycle, a homemade frame holding it together and nothing much to stop you falling out the feeling was somewhat dynamic. It was topped off with a rain cover that looked like it had been made from granny's 1970s' window curtains.

My wife's translation skills were called into action as I wanted to know more about this contraption. Good job she can translate drunken English into Mandarin. She was keen for me to shut up though as it was distracting the driver and this wasn't the best idea as he was mostly going up the road the wrong way, playing what appeared to be 'chicken' with cars and thought nothing of turning across traffic without slowing down or indicating.

But I was having none of it and wanted to know, amongst other things, how he charged it up and how far it would go on a charge. Between asking in English, my wife's translation, the answer in Mandarin and my wife's translation back into English I was leaning rather too far out of the trishaw and happily waving to the locals we passed on the street with a cheery, if somewhat loud, 'nihao' to randomly selected pedestrians. This wasn't only keeping me amused but got responses from most of them ranging from stunned looks to reciprocal waves and giggles at the crazy white guy hanging out of a trishaw.

The answers were back and it appears that from plugging the vehicle into the mains at home for ten hours overnight it'll run for five hours the next day. More than enough for a commute to and from work twice a day for most people. The cost was lower than a petrol-powered version apparently (and easier on the thighs than a traditional pedal-powered model no doubt).

Now this vehicle was obviously something no self-respecting person would drive on the roads; it's a tourist gimmick. But the other motorbikes and some small Chinese branded cars were the exact same models that used petrol engines in other countries and hence you didn't stand out as a tree-hugging lentil-eating lefty with no taste.

So, Xi'an residents seem to be heading towards becoming green even though their industry is somewhat sepia and pumping the sky full of Beijing-rivalling pollution.

There is an ancient industry that's a little more eco friendly here though.

Xi'an is the start of the legendary silk road. It attracted peoples from across the ancient world and to this day there is a strong mix of Middle Asia cultures in the city. It became somewhat rich all those years ago before container ships negated the need for camels to be lugging goods across Middle Asia. It was also the place that held the secret of silk production, hence 'the silk road'.

We went to see a demonstration of how silk thread is made, which involved drowning mulberry silk worms before unravelling their cocoon and twisting eight or so strands into a thread ready for weaving. That was a secret (on pain of death) that stayed with China for a long time and made Xi'an very rich. So they built a city wall to protect the trade and all that wealth.

You can hire a tandem bicycle and pedal round the city's splendidly restored city wall today. So we did. Not round the bottom I hasten to add, but around the top! You're some fifty foot up in the air on a cobbled surface with rampart walls and every so often a period wooden building that was previously a barracks or look-out tower or something like that. This was a wonderful place to view the smog from.

The same seems to be true in Chengdu. This is the place famous for Sichuan spicy food, teahouses, pandas and last year a rather large earthquake. The earthquake didn't hit the city, but did a good job of messing up the nature parks and the pandas' habitat. But I think the biggest threat to their survival is the air pollution. I fear pretty soon our furry friends will be in oxygen tents.

We went to see the giant pandas and their little red cousins which was very enjoyable (if you discount the Chinese tourists with volume control problems). We chose to go to a breeding and research centre as trying to see them in the wild is a very hit and miss affair as they're shy and there aren't many of them left. They're in large open forest areas at the centre but can be counted on to turn up for the cameras at feeding time. So we had lots of lovely pictures of some of the cutest mammals on the planet. You can't help but feel all warm and fuzzy – a response that the WWF no doubt considered when making the giant panda its symbol and mascot.

Marco Polo was famous for bringing the Orient to Europe but equally as famous for never mentioning tea. Thanks to the British a large part of the world probably associates the brew these days more with a small island in the north Atlantic and with India than with China but it's China where the art of tea making really began. Chengdu has some delightful teahouses and a long history with tea so after seeing the pandas we just had to go and try some. What I wasn't expecting was that we'd get an education in making a cuppa.

There are precious few heritage buildings left in Chengdu but if you head to the river you can find a few old-style teahouses. Several give demonstrations of how to make a cup of tea from the dried leaves. We happened upon a small place, with only a couple of tables, where a very charming girl was keen to show her skills. She didn't really speak English but thought I was very handsome so naturally I was keen to hear more. The missus acted as translator again, but as it was a practical demonstration not a lot of words were needed.

We tried three teas in all: Chinese red, black and jasmine. All had distinct tastes that were enhanced by the process of warming the leaves, pouring the first cup away to take away the primary bitter taste and then pouring the cup that was to be drunk. With the setting, the period-costumed tea girl and the high quality of the tea the experience was one I'd recommend you spend an hour enjoying.

Dunking a teabag into a cup of boiling water just won't cut it ever again.

Yak butter and prayer wheels

So we started in Beijing in the north east of China and have made it all the way across country to Lhasa in Tibet, south west China. Quite a trip and one that helps you better view, if not understand, the Chinese nation's foibles and fantastic cultures.

The altitude at just over 3600m above sea level makes you slow down a little and this is generally the first impression I got of the locals. They move a little more sedately than the mainland Chinese. Maybe it's the altitude but there's a good chance that lifestyle has a part in it too. Tibetans appear to be far more overtly religious than the rest of China. The all-out pursuit of cash that you can see in large parts of China isn't obvious in the Tibetans, but the beliefs and actions of a devoutly religious people are. You can't walk ten metres without sniffing incense and having to get out of the way of a swinging battle mace the locals call a prayer wheel. This is a handheld device with a vertical handle, an ornate metal canister (with a prayer sutra inside) that rotates on the top, and a weight on the end of a chain connected to the canister that allows you to maintain rotating momentum when you get going (think handheld swing ball). They can be bought in most local outlets, as most local outlets sell exactly the same things, and make great souvenirs. You can even take them on planes which is odd, as I'd swear they're more lethal than a pair of nail clippers.

Anyway, my observations were picking up a trend. It seems to me that the older the person swinging the wheel the larger it was. There were several little old ladies with leathery skin a rhino would have been proud of toting wheels that large they needed a harness. This may have been to take the weight but could just as easily have been to prevent the person from taking off from centrifugal force. You needed to give these gals a wide berth.

Now, in the west we go to church but in Tibet they go to a temple. You don't just go in, sleep a little, sing a little and come back out though. The believers (who appear to be one hundred per cent of the ethnic Tibetan population) first walk around the temple in a clockwise direction with said prayer wheel. The clockwise direction apparently relates to Buddhism and this is also the direction you spin your wheel in. There is another more ancient religion in Tibet called Bon and these guys go in an anti-clockwise direction, presumably so you can spot them easily as non-Buddhist without the need for costumes, funny hats or flashing lights. Now, here's the thing. They do this daily. The really devout go around prostrating themselves on the floor every step of the way. Then you have the quite frankly insane who will make their way from across the mountains to get to Lhasa's most holy of temples (Jokhang) in this fashion. A damn good way of staying fit no doubt but it makes you wonder how any work gets done.

Now, inside these temples are some of the oldest Buddhas and other religious deities anywhere in the world. There's only one way in and out and it's rather a special experience going in. After first seeing some lovely artwork and doorway adornments as you step into a rather dark entrance, a peculiar smell that isn't incense meets your nostrils immediately. This is then followed by you trying to regain your footing Bambi-style from something slippery on the stone floor. Both sensations come from the same revered substance. Yak butter. Yep, take one yak. Milk it. Shake it around a bit (the milk, not the yak) and you've got the stuff that fires the religious candles of a nation as well as being used to make the most awful tea in the world. The locals can't get enough of the stuff. It's presented as offerings at all temples and when you're inside the lack of air-conditioning, windows or a second exit, combined with yak butter makes you feel a little funky to say the least.

The Potala Palace is significantly less pungent but that's probably because it's the home of the Dalai Lama and he hasn't been home in fifty years. There are priests roaming around and the bodies of most of the previous thirteen Lamas are interned downstairs but this place is bright and breezy and after a recent makeover and lick of paint a rather impressive pile.

Seems the thought of the spiritual leader of the

Buddhist religion residing in such a magnificent and historied palace in Lhasa is too much for the Chinese government to accept though. So he's down the road in India which is where Buddhism started anyway. Pity, as he'd add a little pizzazz to the Tibetan capital.

Walking through the revered man's quarters on the thirteenth floor definitely gives you a sense of spiritual presence. Being surrounded by the history of centuries in the form of mandalas, scripture, artwork and gold is a memorable experience. The seat cushions that were not only where the Dalai Lama sat but also his attending court hadn't even been fluffed so you got the feeling their holy butts had just left the building.

The breeze coming through the window is rather bracing this far up the side of a hill nearly 4000 metres high in the Himalayas too. The only downside to the view, apart from the fact I was expecting snow on the mountains, is the feeling that Lhasa is no longer the place of legend you read about in books and see depicted in the movies. It's turning into just another standard Chinese city in large parts with block upon block of square and soulless concrete buildings.

The growth of Lhasa is largely down to mainland Chinese immigrants. Growth usually brings some benefits which is good but let's hope they realize what a special place exists here before there's little left to differentiate the heart of a unique culture from the backstreets of Chengdu, Xi'an or any other Chinese city you care to name.

Oh yes, the Lhasa skies are a beautiful blue with no sign of pollution and the air is fresh and clean. Now, the day that changes will be a crime.

When not praying, priests are just as human as the rest of us.

Awakening giant

China is a land of over a billion people with many different ethnic ancestries and languages. You'd therefore expect a huge diversity of experience when you visit. And that's what you sort of get. The Han Chinese dominate the sub-continent though and this culture is largely what you see everywhere in today's China. Communism may be the name over the door of the party headquarters but you'll struggle to find a Chinese who doesn't think free enterprise and profit are a good thing.

In my lifetime it's only been the last decade or so that China has been open to the world. In this time it's made massive leaps forward economically but without losing an ancient Confucius past. It's ultra modern in parts and gloriously backward in others. It has some of the most impressive and majestic sights on the planet and a largely unbroken culture stretching over 3000 years.

Everyone has a view on this country whether they've visited or not. That in itself tells you it's worth exploring and I for one will be doing more of that in the years to come. I'm looking forward to experiencing the liberation of a waking giant and their more active role in the wider world. More Chinese power will at least mean we'll all be eating a lot better after all!

New Zealand

New Zealand

The great drawback to New Zealand comes from the feeling that after crossing the world and journeying over so many thousand miles, you have not at all succeeded in getting away from England. (Anthony Trollope, 1873)

Land of the long white cloud

Now as a Brit I should be well qualified to comment here.

I'd agree that they speak English, most places have tea shops and fish and chip takeaways (good ones I might add) and they drive on the correct side of the road. Street names seem ever so familiar and come to that so do some of the town and city names, Christchurch, Canterbury and Cambridge being three easily recognizable ones.

They've also managed to retain the ability to make great meat pies. Now in the grand scheme of culinary inventions, the meat pie must be just above a sandwich but would you believe the missus can't get enough of them.

Nowadays in England, you'll find them being sold in fairly low rent establishments and resembling a large beige coloured hockey puck both in physical shape and texture. You can get them in low rent establishments in New Zealand too but by and large they taste wonderful. There's very little hoof and arsehole in them from what I can tell. Lamb, beef or other such chunks of meat are easily identifiable. Frequently I'll ask the question about what do you fancy for lunch and a smiling face retorts 'meat pie'.

My missus is Singaporean. It's a commonly held belief in Singapore that a large proportion of the local's brain is devoted to food. Bad food in Singapore will close the establishment down before they've finished the washing up. I've lived there for nearly a decade and can attest to just how good the food is. Not a lot of crap passes her lovely lips then so even though I like them too her concurrence confirms my taste buds aren't wrong.

Continuing with the comparative theme I would also observe that there is a politeness to the people, a very community based way of life (if you get out of Auckland) and a feeling that a work/life balance exists. Living in a 24/7 world city it's rather unusual to see the shops closing at 6pm on most days and people going home to their families and/or social lives. I do fondly remember this being the norm in the UK of my youth but not any more.

A bit of a generalization but I also found that there seems to be a conservative approach to development and conservation. People don't need to be told to be 'green' or to consider the environment, it's just what they do naturally. The '100% Pure New Zealand' marketing tag line seems to be true, then. In Britain it just seems to be develop and be damned.

Both Britain and New Zealand have truly beautiful

scenery but there's no contest when it comes to the adjective 'dramatic'; New Zealand wins hands down. It even rains quite a bit (whether it's sunny or not).

So then, that all sounds very familiar. But Mr Trollope is out of date. Britain has moved on and become less British than I'd like to remember. Yes, there are lovely pockets of Britishness to be found in the cities, the countryside and the people that make the UK a lovely place on a sunny day but generally you have to look harder than you did in my youth. The movies are wrong as well. No one wears a bowler hat, drinks tea or eats fish and chips. I'd wager there are more hoodies, coffee drinkers and curry eaters.

The Britain of today is cosmopolitan and somewhat overcrowded with more than 56 million people squeezed on to a small island. New Zealand has about the same space with less than a tenth of the population. I'd say it's just as cosmopolitan as Britain but the lack of people seems to give it an opportunity to retain a more agreeable feel.

New Zealand then seems to be a strong facsimile of a lot of what I remember being good about my home land. So does that make it more British than Britain? Well no, but that's a good thing.

Highways, hobbits and hot pools

The first and last time I was here was nearly a decade ago. A lot of the old 1970s' cars have disappeared and the internet has arrived but most other things seem similar. That's good. I only visited the South Island last time and spent my time tramping and climbing. Tramping by the way is not a career as a homeless person, it's what the Kiwis call trail walking. This time though we're on a self drive for a month throughout the North and South Islands. This means, not only do we get to set our own itinerary but I get to do a lot of driving.

As I mentioned we live in Singapore. A very nice place to reside where it's sunny most days of the year, the locals are friendly, the beer is cold, the weather is warm (sometimes a bit too warm) and the facilities are on par with the world's best cities. It's got nearly five million people on seven hundred square kilometres of land which means it's a little cramped to say the least. The island state's local nickname is 'the little red dot', which refers to the fact that on a map of the world the red dot used to depict a capital city is actually bigger than the country itself. You won't be surprised to hear then that you don't get to drive far before a traffic light, junction or jam stops you. As I said earlier, I'm a petrolhead. This is hence one of the few gripes about my chosen home.

New Zealand has vastly more space and would you believe fewer people. They have ten times more sheep than the four million humans, which makes for plenty of succulent lamb dishes and the odd sheep-shagging joke.

They even have a lake that's the size of Singapore. So this then is a good 'man-to-space' ratio particularly when you are doing the full fat New Zealand driving tour we are. It's even better when you factor in most of the routes we're taking seem to have little to no traffic, the roads are well surfaced (generally) and there are no speed cameras that we saw. Watch out for the radar toting police cruisers though.

Anyhow, I digress. So, that lot would normally be

NEW ZEALAND 37

Did I tell you the one about the furry underwear?

enough for me to be in ecstasy but there's a further element to consider. Most of these roads are not motorways. They are single lane highways. And most of these must have been designed by nature-loving racing drivers as they dip, swoop and weave around, over and through some of the most stunning scenery you'll find anywhere in the world.

Getting into the driver's seat of anything modern with four seats and a two-litre engine is sufficient to get the blood pumping and your concentration turned on. How I wish we could have fitted all the luggage (don't forget we're on a one-year tour) into a two-seat sports car but alas we couldn't. Mental note made to come this way again with a hanky-sized bag and a clean licence.

I won't bore those non-car enthusiasts out there with regaled tales of Nurburgring-esque roads, feathered throttles and smooth transitions but suffice to say if you're into cars this is the country to come to. Anywhere outside the major cities will do but I can particularly recommend the Coromandel Peninsula and the whole of the South Island. All are REALLY worth a squirt of unleaded.

We spent a few days in Rotorua. It rained. It is winter though so I suppose it was likely to. No matter. The locals call this place Rotten-rua. Nope, it's not decaying but there is the sense that several schools have organized the troublemakers into a stink bomb competition. This place is pretty much volcanic and has an air of eau de rotten egg about it. The hydrogen sulphide is somewhat pervasive.

So after seeing the bubbling mud pools and geysers we headed out of town to see if we could find the hobbits. Yep, New Zealand was home to the Lord of the Rings (LOTR) production team for a few years while they made the trilogy and a few sites are still selling tickets to the groupies. The spectacular scenery on the movies is actually real (just the fantastical cities, creatures etc were computer generated) and you don't have to travel far to be in at least one of the regions used. Took us a while to find Hobbiton though (the commercial name given to 'the Shire' where the hobbits lived) as it seems the Kiwis are a little embarrassed by midgets with hairy feet and haven't signposted the place very well. Bloody place was closed by the time we got there too. It's slap bang in the middle of a working sheep farm and there are only two tours a day. We didn't lose any sleep as a large number of the places we were booked to stay in were also locations on the LOTR movies so plenty of time to spot Rivendel, Mordor et al.

The place we stayed at in the Maori cultural centre that is Rotorua was twenty clicks out of town on Lake Rotoiti. Bugger of a place to find several miles down a forest track but by George it was a cracking find. The proprietors were a hoot too. I forgot to mention, we decided on homestays and bed and breakfasts in New Zealand rather than hotels. It's turning out to be a great choice. Far superior views to most hotels you'll find, you get to receive first-hand knowledge on where to go and what to do from the proprietors, and the rates are agreeable too.

The weather was still against us so a suggestion was made that we go see the waterfall and hot pools in the back garden. We figured that must mean twenty metres out the back door but it turned out to be twenty minutes hiking up a track in the rain. 'Just follow the rushing water and scent of a volcano,' said the rather jovial owner.

The missus wanted to stay in bed so I was hoping it wasn't going to be a disappointment. After navigating the gorse, several swampy sections and lots of mud we found it and whilst smaller than expected it was worth the rain-soaked walk. Stripping down in the cold rain to hop into a natural hot pool the same temperature as a hot bath was invigorating. Getting back out again into cold wind and rain was even more so. The whole experience put a smile on the face and a stiffness in the nipples.

There are hot springs popping up all over this area. In fact, there are hot springs popping up throughout a large part of the North Island. Geothermic activity is as common as the stunning scenery on this part of the

Pacific Ring of Fire. A lot have had a hotel, spa or fence put around them and an entrance fee attached. The one we were now sitting in was undiscovered except by the four households who lived on this section of the lake, plus their prior guests. It's nice to know a secret, isn't it?

The really amazing hot pools though were on the beaches. Take a spade, your swimmers and start digging. Specific beaches and spots on those beaches have hot spring water pushing up through the sand. On a cold winter's day on a windswept beach it's quite a thing to see people digging a hole, stripping off, sitting in it and looking happy. Now having done it I can tell you that it's one of life's great free pleasures. Best to stay at least a metre away from the point the water comes up to the surface though, as that spot will hard-boil your testicles.

Maoris, mountains and man juice

Having experienced a good slice of nature we thought it time to look into the cultural side of New Zealand.

You've all seen a rugby game when the All Blacks have played, right? Before the start of the game they perform the Haka. This is a war-like chant and dance that talks about living and dying and being a big man. It's intended to galvanize their team whilst instilling apprehension in the opponents. If you watch it you'll admit I'm sure that it's pretty effective even towards a TV viewer. It's taken from the Maoris, New Zealand's original Polynesian inhabitants with the long tongues, tattooed faces and bulging eyes.

We thought it would be good to see a little Maori

tribal dancing while we were here, and where better than the cultural heartland of Rotorua? Only problem was they didn't seem to want to come out in the rain and cold. I blame it on the attire. Here we were with boots and jackets and all they had was a grass skirt and a spear. Enough to wilt anyone's Haka.

We had a few additional opportunities for a cultural experience on the South Island. The Ngai Tahu tribe call this home and are scattered throughout the island from Invercargill in the deep south to Nelson in the north. We got to find out more when we reached Kaikoura.

This town is on the east coast, between Picton and Christchurch, and hence is on the Pacific Ocean. It has a strong Maori history that goes back to the original tribes who inhabited the island and the traditions are very much kept alive today by the families in the region. We met Maurice whose father, grandfather, great grandfather, great great grandfather, great great great grandfather and a few past uncles had been in charge in the region for a very long time.

He taught us the hongi, the famous nose-touching greeting, and assigned us 'Maori' names that we found out later meant we were numbered from 1 to 4. Oh mirth. Mine was *Wha*, pronounced *Far*. *Wh* is an *F* sound you see. It's used a lot in the Maori language and there are a lot of places in New Zealand beginning with *Wh*. You'd think this would be a little tricky for foreigners but it was easy to remember for both of us as we'd encountered a town on the North Island called Whakapapa that got our attention. Not sure that one was thought through so well, but as I said it's easily memorable.

He also explained the formal way of greeting

someone which involves you explaining which mountain, river and canoe you belong to. Sounds kinda funny to a westerner who would normally give the city and country when asked 'Where are you from?'. Greetings are a little more focused toward nature with the Maoris it seems.

The idea is that it bonds you to the earth and the place you live and identifies who your tribe is. This of course sounds great when you have an impressive 3000-metre mountain in the backyard and the local river is used for whitewater rafting. It's not so impressive a greeting when your mountain is a miniature blot on the landscape and the river is a muddy stream. Some poor bloke from the outback in Australia had to offer up this truth as his greeting. Being based in Singapore wasn't much better as the highest 'peak' is 165m above sea level and the Singapore river isn't exactly the Zambezi.

The canoe bit was also a bit strange to us but was explained on the basis that the original Maori settlers canoed over from Polynesia. So your canoe told people the tribe you were from and which migration wave your family came over with. Again, when asked to advise our 'canoe' the best I could come up with was a Boeing 747 having spent the last twenty years on one. Although you have to admit that's more impressive than a hollowed out tree trunk. Our Aussie friend was now really stumped and could only come up with a Ford truck. Given the rivalry between the Kiwis and the Aussies he was probably thinking by this time that Maurice had made all of this up just to take the piss out of his Antipodean cousins.

Anyway, seems it was one of Maurice's ancestor's ideas to stop whaling and start whale watching. You see, this region is home to many sperm whales and a migratory route for many other whale species. The European whalers got wind of this and soon turned up in the nineteenth century chasing riches. We were here to see the whales too.

I always wondered how the sperm whale ended up with such an unfortunate name. I was provided with an answer on the whale-watching trip. Apparently a sperm whale has two and a half tonnes of oil in its head. When the whalers discovered this they thought it was man juice. Gives a whole new angle to the term dickhead doesn't it! So the whale got a name. Obviously the whalers were wrong and when they figured this out by catching a female who had the same oil, one could imagine how they laughed. But the oil was very valuable in the Victorian age so I guess the laugh was on the poor sperm whale.

The town these days though is famous for watching them. It's also very famous for crayfish. You can eat these, no need for a camera. It's the humble but rather lovely-tasting crayfish that gives the town its name actually. Kaikoura means 'Eat Crayfish' in Maori. See, I've been paying attention. The first Maoris pitched up hungry, went sea fishing and pulled out a few. Turned out to be a meal worth naming the place after. Obviously, they kept the Maori name which sounds better than I think it would in English as 'Eat Crayfish' sounds more like an instruction.

We got four sperm whale sightings on our trip which apparently is good. To be honest, it wouldn't have mattered if we'd seen none because Kaikoura is home to a view that beats just about any other coastal view on the planet. And before you think of one make sure you've been here first. Even then you're probably wrong. By the way, I should say that parts of the world where you need a boat or plane to get to don't count! But even if they did the South Island of New Zealand probably still wins with such incredible contenders as Milford Sound, Doubtful Sound and many other head-shakingly beautiful views in Fiordland and the Southern Alps.

But Kaikoura really is special. Probably why the Maoris stayed. You can drive there and even buy a house with the view I'm talking about. Snow-capped mountains under deep blue skies with a wisp of white cloud seem to come right down to the bay and touch the beach. Even though it was winter when we were there the skies were sunny and the sea calm. And don't forget the whales, sea lions and dolphins frolicking just off shore. We spent the next couple of days driving through and around the mountains and gazed upon spectacular vista after spectacular vista but the sight of Kaikoura didn't leave us.

And the memory of Maurice stuck with us too. He took us on a cultural tour and whilst he didn't have a tattooed face or a grass skirt, and wasn't at all interested in doing a tribal dance for us, he was rather fond of singing and playing the guitar. He'd worked this into the deal and had us all singing an unpronounceable Maori song from the get-go. At one point whilst walking through a very nice forest we seemed to be singing to every large tree we came across. Something about them being sacred but, to be honest, I was starting to feel a little like a hippy. A pleasant afternoon though and a very down to earth introduction to a very interesting people.

Wet Coast madness

The west coast of the South Island is famous for windswept deserted beaches, glaciers that come down to temperate rain forests, millions of sandflies and bugger all people. Oh yeah, it has one of the highest rainfalls of any place on earth too (over nine metres a year). We've been getting a good dose of the yearly quota since we arrived.

That's okay though as you can't expect every day of a year to be sunny and the rain is rather nice when you're properly dressed and there's a beautiful beach or mountain in the picture. 'Yes, the beach is just ten minutes' walk down that track,' says the bloke whose house we're staying in, gesturing into the rain. The mountains and glaciers are also there, we're assured by another proprietor in Franz Josef (the town named for the glacier on its doorstep). The four-day storm is somewhat throwing a shroud over my photo opportunities though.

It does slow down enough for us to take a few hikes around some of the very dramatic coastline. Glaciers coming all the way down the Southern Alps mountain range into a temperate rain forest is rather a beautiful thing to see.

The 'Wet Coast', as I'd decided this part of the South Island should have been named, wasn't without distractions other than the mountain scenery. Both in nature and man-made. I've already mentioned the sandflies. Think giant mosquito with attitude. Get anywhere near a slightly cool and shady beach and the buggers are on you and down to lunch without hesitation. Unlike mosquitoes that sneak up, grab a quick snack and disappear before you generally know they're there, sandflies sit around for a full three-course meal. They're enjoying themselves that much that they forget to fly away when you spot them and then kill them with a smack. There are so many of them though that I can only assume the mortality rate from humans swatting them during dessert doesn't do much to bring about extinction. Tried putting on several types of insect repellent but nothing seemed to stop them. It wasn't until the day we left New Zealand that a lady taxi driver of advanced years told me I should have used a mixture of witch hazel and olive oil. 'They hate the smell,' I was reliably informed. Looking down at my red spotted legs from many a sandfly feast I couldn't help but wonder where this woman had been for the last month.

Now, the rain was still coming down, the wind was still blowing and with the windy roads down here you needed to keep vigilant as a sharp corner or precipitous drop was usually only a short distance away. But the next surprise was neither. We'd been following a coastal stretch that was narrow and had a railway line running next to the road for several miles. Then the two met. Now, there are railway crossings all over the world, but this wasn't a crossing. When I say they met, what I meant is that they merged. On a single lane bridge. Not one lane in each direction I hasten to clarify, but *one* lane. This means only one vehicle in one direction at any one time. Whether it be car or train. No traffic lights to determine priority either, although one would assume that if a train was coming it would probably be best to let it go first. Mmmmm!

A little further down the road you come across similar lunacy with roundabouts. The railway cuts straight through the middle of these.

Now look, I'm all for a bit of fun on the roads and applaud common sense applied to any problem in life but with all this space couldn't they have separated them? I've heard of saving money by not spending unnecessarily but this seems like a budget cut too far. Perhaps it's a tourist gimmick. After all, I am writing about it!

Having survived the west coast we headed inland and south. Wanaka was glorious and Queenstown another scenic gem. We kept going all the way down to the south coast where the next major land mass is Antarctica. We skied, we drank in the continuing glorious views and of course the local wines, and as the sun shone on the first day of spring we were really getting lost in ourselves and our fledgling journey.

Crazy Kiwis

There are lots of beautiful lakes on the inland side of the Southern Alps. Lake Tekapo overlooks New Zealand's tallest mountain, Aoraki Mount Cook. Lake Wanaka overlooks Mount Aspiring and Lake Te Anau overlooks the Murchison and Kepler ranges of Fiordland. All stunning, stunning, stunning.

Lake Wakatipu overlooks a range of mountains too. If you've seen the view across Lake Wakatipu you'd agree that whilst this is also stunning a better description could be 'remarkable'. The lake is long and narrow. The mountain range seems to sit close on the far shore, which is actually very close indeed, and is sprinkled with snow. It is long and fairly uniform in impressive height and disappears off into the distance south along the lake. I guess the original settlers thought the description a good one too as this range is called 'The Remarkables'. No less than Sir Edmund Hillary used to climb here in preparation for scaling Mount Everest.

A Mr William Gilbert Rees founded Queenstown in 1861. There's a statue of him on the waterfront of Lake Wakatipu with a very happy looking sheep. Shortly after he pitched up and set up a farm it was also the site of the largest gold rush in the southern hemisphere.

After being a sleepy resort destination for a handful of locals for a long while there's now a new gold rush in the form of tourists and their dollars. For a destination in the middle of nowhere at the end of the earth (from most of the world's perspective) this town certainly has a lot going on. Nightlife, adventure sports, water sports, skiing, handgliding and scenic flights are just a few of the things you can lighten your wallet with.

When we got to town the place was full of queens. Quite apt. These queens weren't here for a beauty pageant though and they also weren't visiting royalty. They were largely from Australia. To be precise Sydney. Gay Ski Week is apparently a leading event in Queenstown. As the weather was sunny and windless we decided to take to the slopes too. Now, when we came to New Zealand I never thought we'd go skiing so much. Partly because the missus had never done it before and was a little apprehensive (but believe me she's taken to it quickly) and partly because I figured we wouldn't be blessed with such good weather. Then again, if someone had told me I'd have been skiing in the middle of a sausage fest I wouldn't have thought that either.

Local inventions fuelled this remote town being dubbed 'The adventure capital of the world'. Sir William Hamilton and A J Hackett respectively came up with the jet boat and bungy jump. The former was invented to allow farmers and settlers to travel up difficult river sections. The latter was purely for an adrenalin rush. Both are rather a hoot when you strap tourists to them and plunge them into the canyons and rivers around town.

A jet boat is a wonderful invention. Its propeller (correctly called an impeller) is inside the hull of the boat which means there are no parts underneath the hull (important this!). Water is sucked into it from the underside of the boat and squirted at 800 litres a second out the back. A bloody great V8 engine with the grunt of a Ferrari is normally the power source. The performance is like a Ferrari too both in terms of acceleration and handling. The most fascinating aspect of this crazy boat though is it only needs 25cm of water to operate on (no parts under the boat to hit the bottom you see). That's basically a puddle. The power of the water jet coming out the back can be directed with a nozzle and this makes it extremely manoevurable. Time for a ride then.

After getting you kitted out in a life jacket (one of the staff quipping with Kiwi aplomb that if we fell out we should spend the time in the water searching around on the river bed for gold as the Shotover river had lots) and what felt like Harry Potter's wizard's cloak (to keep us dry apparently (yeah right)), we got into the boat while it was fighting against the rushing whitewater river. A ten-second unintelligible pep talk from the driver later and we're careering along at a fair old clip only inches from the river bank. The river bank is made of rock and is about fifty metres high. Your sphincter is a pretty good gauge of distance under such circumstances I find.

The rapids are launching great plumes of water into your seat and the wind chill is giving you brain freeze between your eyes. And then the driver does a 360-degree turn. Think Formula 1 driver performing a 'doughnut' for the crowds. Twenty minutes of this and you're either ready for the toilet or a warm bath. We loved every second!

Mr Hackett made himself famous by jumping off the Eiffel Tower with his feet attached to an elastic band. Got himself arrested but started a crazy adrenalin rush sport that most have now heard of. Thirty years later and there are numerous 'bungy' sites around the world but the originals are in Queenstown.

There are several to choose from.

Would Sir like to tie his feet to a rubber band and launch himself off a mountain side? Wonderful view of Queenstown. Or perhaps off a bridge and have a refreshing ice-cold head plunge into the river below? No? Then can we offer you the chance to drop 134 metres (it takes eight seconds you know) from a gondola strung up on wires between two mountains? If you look closely on the way down you might be able to see whitewater rafters waving at you as they bob along the Nevis river.

Sounds vaguely bizarre being offered a menu of ways in which to loosen your bowels and make a screaming girl out of you. I mean, why would you do such a thing?

Well, a teenager might see this as a way of getting laid. One of the male staff actually told me all he had to do was tell his chosen target that he worked for the local bungy operator and tonight would be a happy one.

That argument's no good for me though. I'm a happily married man with not a lot I feel I need to prove to anyone. Plus, just thinking about the idea gives you a primeval urge to stay safe and say hell no. Best to find something more leisurely to do then.

Well no. I went for the lot.

There's a marked difference between the general demeanour of one about to jump and one who's jumped. The former is usually quiet or a little nervous. Most have an expression on their face of being deep in thought about something. I wonder what.

Upon arrival at the jump site a large number head straight to the toilet. It seems adrenalin is brown after all!

Afterwards, it's all high fives, smiles, grand adjectives and joy.

While you're standing waiting for your turn (oh yes, there's a queue. Not only do you part with a sizeable wedge of cash to do this but you have to wait in line) you start sizing up the drop, squinting to see if the ropes are properly attached and trying to reaffirm that this is a good thing to do today.

When you get to the jump point on the bridge, ledge or gondola there's a hive of activity as the crew reconfirm your weight to make sure the bungy is the right length (wouldn't want you bungying too close to terra firma), get you strapped into a harness and bind your feet together. The latter is surprisingly very low tech for such a seemingly dangerous pastime. I could swear I've got a bath towel at home just like the one he's wrapping my feet in and that strap and velcro is straight off a rucksack. But it's too late now, you're committed. Time to be a man and get on with it.

The crew are now asking you to wave at the crowd

and the cameras. Standing on a ledge the size of a tea tray, your main concern at this precise point in time is the bungy equivalent of premature ejaculation. You really don't want to go too soon.

It didn't look so far down fifteen minutes ago.

Okay, 5-4-3-2-1 go! At this point you're, quite surprisingly, executing a swan dive an Olympian would be proud of (the video a wee bit later did confirm it wasn't a bad effort!) whilst screaming like someone had just poured hot water down your pants and noticing through bulging eyes that the ground is rushing up to meet you rather quickly. The bungy cords, plus a few parts of your anatomy, tighten and before you have time to figure out which way is up you're heading skyward.

Launch point, sky, crowd, rock, earth and river alternate for a few more seconds before the bunge has gone from your bungy and it's time for them to retrieve you. You can now wave to the crowds and officially swap over into confident swagger mode.

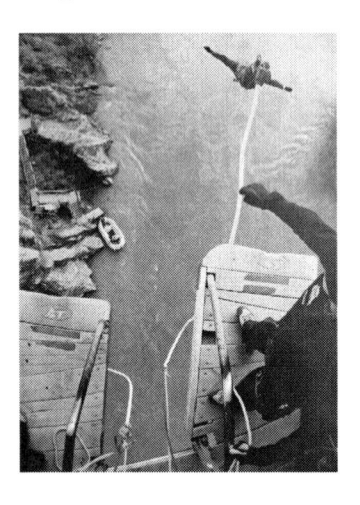

It's like falling off a log. That's attached to the top of a rather tall tree.

So where the bloody hell is everyone?

So there you have it. New Zealand.

Scenery to die for, roads to get nicked for, plenty of space to stretch out in, food and drink that will put a smile on your face, locals with a sense of humour, quirky sports and they speak English to boot. So why are only four million people living here? Who cares? Like the locals, keep it to yourself and enjoy.

Australia

Australia

Eat or be eaten

'Come to Australia, you might accidentally get killed. Your blood will definitely be spilled ...' was the opening ditty of a song on the car stereo.

Now, the Aussies and English (or Poms as the Aussies affectionately like to call us) have a history of fierce competitiveness and general ribbing, which probably dates back to the first people to be incarcerated in the British prison that was Australia, but this is going too far methinks! My initial fears of reprisal due to the recent rugby and cricket wins for my homeland were unfounded as the song unfolded though. Seems it's the wildlife you need to watch out for. The song goes on to list a whole host of God's own that will bite, sting, stab or just generally fuck up your day.

But it's not as bad as it seems as the beasties are harder to find than the media would have you believe, whether on land or in the water. Which whilst denting your ability to regale tales of encounters with the weird and dangerous at future dinner parties does somewhat increase the probability of you actually being at the dinner party. It's easier to find whales, dolphins and turtles (just go to the Whitsundays) than it is to see sharks, blue ringed octopuses and box jelly fish. Which is a good thing. The former are cute and friendly. People make furry toys in their image. The latter are more likely to be on a warning sign on the beach.

There are also signs along the roads and in the bush for all manner of antipodean oddities you should be careful not to run over or step on but in traversing the country by plane and covering over five thousand kilometres in several rental cars we hardly saw one.

'It's too bloody hot mate,' ventured a guide we'd hired in the Northern Territory. 'You lot are the only ones daft enough to be out in this heat,' he continued. Seems the adage 'Mad dogs and Englishmen go out in the midday sun' is probably true then. But it's not just the Poms apparently. The guide was rather keen to know if there were any Americans or Germans in the small tour group we'd joined. I could only hear Aussies and Brits from the sounds of the voices responding. Oh, and a Singaporean of course. To which he added, 'Aw, in that case you'll be all right then. It's usually those blokes that get killed.' Couldn't help but ask why.

Seems they like to get too close to the snakes, spiders and other generally lethal fauna so as to get a better photo. The result is usually a visit to the local hospital for an average of two tourists a year. Or the morgue. Much better odds than crossing a highway at rush hour but probably still best to wear long trousers and boots, keep one's fingers out of dark places and avoid buddying up with a Yank or a Kraut.

The guide's initial talk did include a rather lengthy discussion on what not to touch, approach or try and feed which had the creeping effect of making you a little bit more jumpy than you would otherwise have been. For example, I started to develop an obsessive compulsive disorder of a morning for footwear checking. This involved me gingerly turning my boots upside down and shaking them vigorously and then poking a stick into the toes and wiggling it. Apparently spiders like the toe area for a snooze. Which would be okay if they were the little non-poisonous variety found in most of Europe. But of course they're not. They're black widows, huntsman or red-backs and will make you rather ill at best and probably kill you painfully at worst. I'm a great fan of espresso coffee, but no cup of hot brown can ensure you're more alert than a paranoia of finding a nasty eight-legged surprise in your personal effects.

I would go through my routine whilst also keeping an eye on the area surrounding our camp for taipans and other deadly serpents. Poisonous snakes were not on my list of antipodean creatures I wanted to see. Humans, it seems, are not on theirs either, as snakes apparently try and give you a wide berth. So as long as you don't accidentally step on one, shove your arm into its hidey hole or ask it to pose for a photo you'll probably live to tell the tale.

So it is that after a few days out in the red centre (which gets its name from the iron oxide in the earth that turns everything that lovely shade of red you instinctively associate Australia with in photos) you start to revert to a more relaxed state and not worry so much about the potential hazards. Take the missus. She generally puts a hot shower at the end of a sweaty day hiking above breathing in terms of priority, so it didn't surprise me too much when she shared one with a huntsman *and* a red-back. They wouldn't move apparently.

Such things shouldn't put you off though as it's definitely worth the coming out here if you're in the country. It's the middle of Australia and that makes it the middle of nowhere too but there's a big rock that's worth the trip alone. Uluru, also known as Ayers Rock, is a very impressive monolith that turns red with the rising and setting sun. I generally like climbing rocks but the local Aborigines discourage this with Uluru as it's considered sacred. This didn't stop a lot of tourists making the ascent but it did contribute to our decision not to. The other factor was that it was forty degrees Celsius outside and it was only eight in the morning. We took a helicopter flight instead which was truly spectacular and gave a perspective of this geological oddity that you just can't get from the ground. And after coming all this way you may as well shell out for the flight as there's nothing else out here to see except seemingly endless desert.

Well, that's not strictly true as the blokes in short pants and long socks in Alice Springs are worth a smile and some of the shops are too. We found one that was selling a videotape called 'How to crack a stockwhip'. Potentially the title of an S&M porn story maybe but on closer inspection it really was a lesson in how to use a whip, to herd animals. Notice I said videotape and not DVD?!

It's also the place where I met my first kangaroo. He was served up with a delicious sweet potato mash and a cheeky Shiraz. Lovely, but not how I expected my first encounter to be. I was hoping to see several bounding across the open plains whilst hearing a faint rendering of 'Skippy, Skippy, Skippy, the bush kangaroo' in the background. No such luck. In fact, the steak wasn't the only part of the animal I got to see before a whole one presented itself. I'm not really thinking road kill when I say this, but there is an awful lot of that. Would you believe you can buy all sorts of kangaroo souvenirs made from various parts of the animal. These range from slippers to coin pouches made out of their scrotums. It still looks like a scrotum too (thankfully with the pubes removed). I know you might as well use the whole animal if you've already killed it for meat and fur but you really have to ask yourself who would buy such tat.

My brother loves the one I got him.

Now, they say kangaroos are a pest and are a danger to humans. Farmers want them culled to prevent crop damage and should you happen to drive into one he could end up on your lap and you and he will be upside down in a ditch at the side of the road. But the ones we saw seemed like very loveable things. So I couldn't help think that this antipodean icon, to be found on the national airline's logo and generally synonymous with the country, is getting a bit of a raw deal.

It's still considered special enough to adorn one half of Australia's national crest which is only right as it's about as Australian as you can get. The other half has an emu on it. As one of my Aussie mates likes to point out, Australia is a country which sees fit to eat both of the animals on its national crest. So I ordered an emu salad the next night. Also a rather nice meal and not at all like chicken.

I didn't feel I was getting even with the man killers that Australia is famous for though. Roos and emus I'm pretty certain don't kill humans either in defence or because they're hungry. So, maybe a snake? I'd eaten a snake in Kowloon a few years back, quite by accident. I hasten to add it was in a restaurant and had been cooked, just seconds after they'd beheaded and skinned it in front of me. I made a mental note to ask for a translation before ordering in future and also not to eat another one. So no snake then.

I've also eaten shark. Both in Asia, where they have a craving for the fins, and Trinidad where it comes in a burger bun and is delightfully called 'shark and bake'. I try not to eat it any more though as there's a bit of a problem with them becoming rare and that's just bad form. So what does that leave? Well spiders of course. Well no. There isn't a lot of meat on a spider and they really don't look particularly appetizing so I wasn't about to eat a spider.

How about a koala? That cuddly marsupial generally to be found sleeping up a gum tree. I know where you think this line is going but no I didn't eat one of those. They may stink of eucalyptus-scented shit but that's not a good enough reason for pan frying one. They're far too cute and rare to accompany your green beans and roast potatoes. Besides, no one had them on the menu.

So I ate a crocodile. Not a whole one I hasten to add, just a steak. Surprisingly delicious, and not at all like chicken either.

I never got to see one of these in the wild. This was probably because we never made it to the far north where I'm told they're bigger than a car and will use your arm as a toothpick just after dining on the rest of you. Good job I beat this croc to the punch then. But I don't think the one that sacrificed itself for my dinner was from there anyway. I'm pretty certain my beasty had been farmed. Probably for its skin for leather goods but as I said earlier, if you're going to kill an animal you might as well use all the bits. And if there's profit in it for the farmer then you can guarantee croc numbers will increase. Which is good, because I could eat this again.

Now at this point you're probably thinking you need to fly to the middle of nowhere, drive for several hours and search out either an aboriginal barbeque or the rickety old local watering hole of an outback settlement to sample such food. Not at all. I guarantee you can find one of the above, or possibly all three, in many a restaurant in the big cities. Queensland excepted. In this state it's apparently okay for the croc to eat you but you can't eat it!

Roos, emus and crocs then. All very tasty, all in plentiful supply and all a very nice change from an Angus beef steak. Give it a go as I think you'll like it. I bet they don't fart as much methane as cows either so maybe you're also helping keep greenhouse gases down by ordering one.

A drop of the clear stuff

It's hot in Australia. I've had a few experiences to confirm just how toasty over the years. Not enough sun cream on your face gives you an interesting red panda look if like me you leave your sunglasses on too long. I've also had my walking boot soles ungluing themselves from the uppers after a few days in the bush due to the sand's temperature. Go sit in a car that's been out in the sun whilst you've been eating lunch and when you get back in you'll be burning your arse on the fake leather car seat. But these are experiences you can have happen to you in the tropics too. What is different to the tropics is that there are two ingredients missing. An ozone layer and regular rain.

The former means you can cook your head on a seemingly cold but sunny day if you don't wear a hat and the latter results in a lot of desert. So much desert in fact that you can now find more camels in Australia than they have in the Middle East!

The desert isn't somewhere that millions of people willingly choose to live if there's a choice. You only need look at a map of Oz and you can see that most of the population live around the edges of the country where there's a river and a bit of breeze.

The rivers in Melbourne, Adelaide and Perth are lovely places to sit back and enjoy a cold beer or chilled white on a sunny day. We found ourselves doing just that in all three places recently and when you throw in a lazy lunch with friends it's even better. Same goes for the harbour in Sydney. Lovely.

However, there's trouble afoot.

Australia has been an attractive place to emigrate to for a long time. My mum did just that in the 1960s. She didn't stay ultimately, which is why I'm a Pom, but always blamed getting married to a non-Australian for that. My first trip to Sydney, a decade ago, to see what all the fuss was about confirmed that she had indeed picked a city that made you smile. Beautiful beaches, a stunning natural harbour and a couple of modern man-made wonders in the form of the opera house and bridge make for an attractive place to set down. Whether you're viewing all this from a bar, a boat or the top of the Sydney harbour bridge doesn't matter, it's special. Very few who travel here return home with a bad report card.

The problem though is that more and more aren't returning home and are instead staying. The infrastructure is creaking as a result. This is most obvious in the traffic jams you're stuck in daily and the bans on using water for washing or watering anything but yourself.

We saw government signs in every village, town and city we went to stating the level of water available at that time. Mostly it said 'moderate'. This has resulted in virtually all regions banning car washing and lawn watering for the majority of the year. We even saw one sign that said 'Don't spit, you might need it!'

Now, as a tourist this is more of an amusing anecdote than a concern but as a resident I'd imagine it's an uncomfortable truth that a country with so much natural wealth (minerals, metals, precious stones, fossil fuels, you name it they've got the lot) can't provide its residents with the one commodity they really need.

I was in Israel a few years back and a local business colleague was banging on about how Israel, a land with very little water, was an exporter of the stuff. I wasn't aware Israel, which is a rather dry area of the Middle East, sold water so was keen to understand the statement. What he was getting at was they grow fruit and vegetables for export. The water was 'put' into the oranges, tomatoes and other plants and sent overseas. 'Why?', was his question.

Australia, like most countries actually, does the same. Australian lamb and beef can be found in most restaurants. I don't just mean the ones in Australia either. Aussie beef and lamb are international brands in their own right. It's lovely too especially when you wash it down with a nice bottle of red. They export that in large quantities as well. Both the animal and the booze need rather a lot of water to create. Many thousands of litres in fact. You can go and look it up on the web.

But hey, why bother 'filtering it' through an animal or a fruit when you can just stick it in bottles and sell it direct without the bothersome fruit, veg and farmyard animals slowing the process down? But shouldn't this be considered lunacy when it's clear the country doesn't have enough?

Such is the profit to be made out of a resource that is as vital to us as air though that I guess it's just too tempting to shoot oneself in the foot. But there is hope it seems in the form of a small town in New South Wales. Bundanoon. This place has only 2500 residents but they've said no to the businessmen tapping their aquifer for profit. In fact they've gone a step further and banned bottled water. They've put up a few taps in town and invite you to bring a bottle and fill up for free.

Wonderful I say. I grew up drinking tap water and considered it more than adequate to hydrate me. The thought of buying bottled water never crossed my mind until I went to a country where the tap variety would result in you making a rapid trip to the loo. Australia isn't one of these by the way. I mean, why would you pay up to five dollars (in many restaurants I could name) for something you can get for less than a penny out of a tap? Perhaps we've all become too rich and regressed into naivety to ask such an obvious question. After all, a bottle of water is now more expensive than the same volume of gasoline for your car, and we're still buying it!

When you consider that fuel has to be dug out of the ground in the form of crude oil (usually from a very inaccessible area, sometimes the ocean) and then processed at great expense before being shipped to where it's needed and dispensed through a further expensive process it's ridiculous. But hey, if we're daft enough to buy it then someone will supply it.

I was pleased to see that virtually all of the lunch and dinner outlets we frequented in Oz offered tap water as an option to the bottled variety without being asked. For free I would add. Those that didn't had to deal with the missus who saw it as an affront to civil rights. Which is a fairly reasonable reaction methinks. Think about it for a few seconds. You're paying a king's ransom for something that is virtually the same as the one being offered for free (or near free, per litre drunk, if you're paying the water rates bill).

So, a little town in New South Wales is hopefully going to start a revolution to take all Aussies back to the good old days of drinking water coming from a tap. I'm personally hoping that this trend spreads worldwide rapidly. Common sense has historically been an Aussie stalwart so my hopes are high.

Van Diemen's Land

It turned out that we'd have to leave mainland Australia before we'd get to see some of Australia's unique wildlife actually in the wild. So it was that we found ourselves in Tasmania. Abel Tasman, a Dutch explorer, who had already been kicked out of New Zealand by the Maoris (but not before he discovered the South Island), discovered it in the 1640s and named it Van Diemen's Land after his then Dutch East Indies Governor. It later got renamed after the founder himself. Fair dinkum as the locals would say.

Now, most people only know Tasmania for two things. The finish line for the Sydney to Hobart yacht race and the devil. I don't mean Beelzebub by the way, I'm talking about a marsupial.

We arrived in Hobart and found our digs up on a hill in Lindisfarne (a suburb of Hobart on the opposite side of the natural harbour to the city centre). Fantastic view of the very pleasant city, Mount Wellington, Mount Nelson, the harbour and its unusual bridge.

The view soon disappeared a day later though as the rains descended but undeterred we figured the wildlife wouldn't care about a spot of rain and we were right. We were heading to a wildlife park to see Tasmanian devils.

Now I know I said we saw a lot of Aussie wildlife in the wild in Tasmania but with the devil you have next to no chance of seeing one unless you go to a conservation park where they're bred. This creature is the largest meat-eating marsupial on the planet but that's not saying much as they're only about the size of a King Charles spaniel and there aren't many meat-eating marsupials. It's like being the fastest snail on the planet or the smallest cat. Yes it's a fact but no, it's not really interesting. Seems the marketing boys didn't have much to work with and when you consider some of its other attributes going with 'largest meat-eating marsupial' was probably the only choice. You see, this poor little waif has got bad eyesight, can't run fast enough to really catch anything, has a poor sense of smell, can't climb and got hit with the stupid stick a lot. In Darwinian terms it's an evolutionary dead end. Tasmania's very own Dodo in the making. And that's why you can't see them in the wild (they'll be extinct, in the wild, within fifteen years according to the ranger we spoke to).

They sleep a lot too so can't be relied upon to

entertain except when feeding time comes around. This is when you get to see why they're called devils. They make a very unearthly sound when fighting each other for food and have a bite force that a saltwater crocodile would be proud of. Every chew of their lunch gives a loud crunch as they demolish the bones, sinew and meat all in one go. They're not picky eaters, these boys. You can also see for yourself that their eyesight and sense of smell are crap as there's lots of food being thrown to them but unless it hits them on the nose they take for ever to find it. Probably the reason why they eat a lot of road kill. With bad eyesight and a turn of speed a chihuahua would mock this sometimes turns out to be their last dining decision.

You've all seen the Warner Bros Tasmanian Devil cartoon, right? Well, after a few minutes observing the real life devils, at feeding time, you can see that whoever created Tassie is pretty close on a few characteristics. They're like a kid that's been given too much sugar. Twisting and turning, snuffling around, changing direction rapidly and all the time making a noise that is somewhere between Maria Sharapova's forehand grunt (on high speed playback) and a hedgehog humping. A curious wee beasty this one.

And he's not alone.

Take the duck-billed platypus. A mammal with a beak, that lays eggs. I remember reading an article somewhere which said that when this creature was first discovered and described in a journal everyone thought the author had made it up. Before reaching Tasmania I'd only ever seen one in a zoo. By the time we left I was still in the same position. Hey ho.

We did get to see kangaroos, wallabies and possums in the wild though. And the odd kookaburra. Oh and

Oh, the indignity of it ...

a wombat. Although that was dead. It's like a giant hamster with tiny eyes and buck teeth. This one was also upside down, a little bloated and had bright white balls. Not sure if they all have bright white balls or if they turn this colour as a result of impending death from a collision with a car but it made for rather a humorous photo nonetheless.

Tasmania is a very nice place to visit and a surprise alternative to the mainland. It's got world-class scenery, friendly locals, nice wines, plenty of water and has given us the chance to tick off another one of the most southerly land masses on the planet that you can visit before you hit Antarctica. It's called Cockle Creek and has a very nice Southern Right Whale sculpture to mark the spot.

A Golden Gaytime

When you think Australia you probably think kangaroos, koalas, surfing, rugby, barbeques, people saying 'G'day cobber', the great barrier reef, an opera house and a harbour bridge.

You may also add Dame Edna Everage, Kylie and Sydney's large gay population to today's Aussie stereotype. The butch stockman image of years gone by has been infiltrated by pop princesses and several cocks in gold lamé frocks.

Most of the big cities we visited have also replaced the boozers with wine bars and the low rent cafés with bistros and the like. Get into the one-horse towns dotted through the expanses of the interstate highway system and you'll still find a boozer but generally the coffee shops and cafés are more noticeable. The Ute has become more of a lifestyle vehicle too (more surfboards in the back than sheepdogs) and there's not a corked hat anywhere to be seen.

The point is that there are many Aussie icons and brands we all know. Some remain constant like Bondi Beach and surfing, some become more noticeable like the Aborigines and some fade away like INXS. And then you have an odd one that makes you wonder, What the ...?

'Golden Gaytime' is one of those.

This sounds like something you could only get in certain suburbs of Sydney but I assure you it's as easy to get as a stubby. The double entendre was intended. What I'm actually referring to though is a bottle of beer and not a fledgling hard-on.

What a brand hey. There aren't many left on the market that leave themselves open to such blatant

'Carry On ...', 'Ooh missus' Frankie Howerd style abuse but the Golden Gaytime just sucks it up (oops!). It's an oldie but a goodie.

So what is it? Well, it's a humble lollipop that's enjoyed by all it seems and it's been around for a very long time. I can only assume long enough for the word 'gay' to have changed its popular meaning from 'happy' to 'homosexual'. But it persists and I've yet to meet an Aussie (hetero, metro or other) who doesn't know what it is and can tell you without a hint of a smirk that they 'love a Golden Gaytime'. I have to say, I'm hooked too. I normally choose a Magnum but I've been seduced during our sojourn down under. With a mixture of vanilla and caramel ice cream covered in chocolate and sprinkled with hokey pokey (honeycomb) it's hard to resist.

Deep blue poo

A trip to Australia without a dip in the ocean would be like going to New York and not bothering to see the Empire State Building. Being so accessible, as virtually everyone lives around the coast, you don't really have a good argument for not going.

One of my friends at this point of the conversation would probably point out that there are sharks out there and that just last week someone was eaten but honestly, you've got significantly more chance of drowning in your own vomit than becoming a Great White's next meal. So take the plunge.

You can of course simply follow the weekend crowd, go down to one of the numerous seaside resorts, strip down to your budgie smugglers (if you're Brazilian) or boardies and dive in. This is a must with such beautiful beaches throughout the coastal areas. If you're allergic to sea water, can't swim or remain convinced there's a shark out there waiting for you then you can even just go and have a look, but go you must. Many bays and beaches have beautifully placed bars to take in the view (Icebergs at Bondi is one of my favourites) and places like the 12 Apostles along the Great Ocean Road in Victoria have walkways and scenic photo points for you to make the most of your visit.

The Great Ocean Road, by the way, takes a couple of days to drive. You can do it faster but won't have gone along the full length in daylight. You may also be stopped from doing it in a day by the police who enforce the speed limit with religious zeal, or other road users who have no intention of letting faster cars past on the mostly single lane coastal highway. So taking two days is what we did. The one area that stands out is that around Port Campbell which is where the famous 12 Apostles sea stacks are. It's a great vista but unfortunately no one has built a bar from which to enjoy it.

If like me though, looking at the deep blue or dipping your toes in at the beach isn't enough then you need to get into it properly. I also need to throw in an activity too as water on its own isn't much fun unless you're skiing or surfing on it or looking under it at the sea life. A beautiful spot with a reef is best for me and Australia just happens to have the world's largest: the Great Barrier Reef.

So it was that we found ourselves in the Whitsunday Islands off the Northern Queensland coast.

There's an advert for Tourism Australia where a stunning white sand beach with turquoise waters and an even more stunning inlet is shown from an aerial view. That's the Whitsundays. Well, more correctly that's one specific piece of Whitsunday Island. The rest of the island and its chain are very nice but this is the bit you want to see.

We're chartering a boat and, even more excitingly, meeting up with some friends. All three are Aussies, all were at our wedding and all are great fun. They're the sort of friends that you don't need to reacquaint with when you've not seen them for a while. You just start talking as though you were with each other yesterday. Effortless, easy and pleasurable. So we have the makings of a wonderful week. This turns out to be even more wonderful on arrival as they've thoughtfully turned up with enough booze to sink the boat. We've got a 36-foot motor yacht that's none too shabby and whilst compact it's more than sufficient to house us in reasonable comfort.

It's too late to leave the safety of our moorings today as whilst the three of them arrived early from Melbourne and Sydney, me and the missus couldn't get a connecting flight from Hobart that got us to Proserpine until late afternoon. It's hence too late to motor off by the time we've transferred to Airlie Beach as quite sensibly, the charter company doesn't let you drive after dark.

So we turn on the barbeque, open a bottle of chilled white and have a chat about where we're going to go and who's doing what on board. Me, plus one of the gang (who's also an amateur pilot) have had some previous boating experience so we should be fine. With an airline stewardess on board and an employee of *National Geographic* we should be okay with safety demonstrations and navigation too!

It still makes me shake my head in wonder though that with barely an hour's tuition (and no driving licence) you can disappear off into the wide blue yonder in a rented rich man's toy and no one bats an eyelid. Then again, as we're the ones about to do this I'm not complaining. It's rather exciting to be back on a boat again and in such a beautiful place. When you're skippering, crewing and looking after yourselves with no hired crew you get such a wonderful sense of freedom. It's just like the freedom you feel when you buy your first car and drive off with your mates for the first time. Splendid.

Watching the sun go down is quite unusual today. A few days ago a red sandstorm turned Sydney into a scene from Mars. You'd have sworn the photos in the newspapers had been taken with a bright orange filter but as two of the three friends are Sydneysiders we're assured it really did look like that. The remnants of that storm are unfortunately with us in Queensland today. Makes for interesting photos. We're too busy cooking, drinking, talking and laughing to really care whether it's orange, blue or green to be honest though.

The next couple of days see us working like a well-oiled machine. Everyone is pitching in, we're all learning to drive, anchor, radio, stow and not use too much water or loo roll. You could have sworn we'd done this together before, but amazingly we haven't. The sun's shining, the haze has cleared to reveal fluffy white clouds and blue sky and we've found a mooring off a beautiful beach with coral only feet below the water.

There's a problem out here with inexperienced sailors hitting the seabed. Just the other day we were having brunch and listening to the ship-to-shore radio and heard a couple of ladies telling the shore controller that they were in about one metre of water and what should they do. Get into deeper water was the obvious retort. I wondered if they'd been drinking a little too much of a local beer called 'Pure Blonde'. So, not wanting to add to the statistics we take extra care to stay away from the shallows and use our dinghy to transport us and our snorkel gear in.

I used to scuba dive in years gone by but stopped for no really solid reason that I can think of as it's a wonderful world down below. Such incredible colours, shapes and designs of life you could never see on the surface. And just like us landlubbers it needs sunlight. This means that a lot of interesting stuff is just below the surface so you actually don't need to go to the trouble of getting kitted up to dive you can just snorkel, and snorkelling on a reef is a great place to see fish, coral and crustaceans up close.

One of my favourites is the parrot fish. I love the way they seem to fly through the water with their fins flapping almost like the wings of a bird. They're also very brightly coloured with a palette that covers the visible light spectrum and some interesting variations of shade and design on individual fish too. They eat coral. You can hear this when your head is in the water. It sounds like chipping away at a limestone rock with a pair of pincers, which is pretty close to exactly what is happening as parrot fish have a beak very similar to a parrot (hence the name).

Which leads me to the beach.

Pure white sand, that in many a book would be described as being like caster sugar. Well it isn't, it's parrot fish poo! Okay there's shell in there too and a few ocean rolled pebbles and the like but a large part of white sand is delivered to the beach via the backside of a parrot fish. That chomping that you can hear when your head is underwater is the fish demolishing the coral. The hard, calcified part of the coral can't be consumed so a while later it's squirted out the back. This is equivalent to a kilogram each day, which is ironically about the same weight as a bag of sugar. There's a lot of fish here so, hey presto the beaches are kept well stocked.

We'd got the beers out and were messing about on the sand when the inevitable happened and one of the girls commented that the sand was 'just stunning. So pure, so clean and fresh looking, it feels lovely between your toes'. So I couldn't resist telling. Of course they didn't believe me and figured I was winding them up, until later that day we were back on the boat and I handed round one of the sea life books we'd got onboard. I guess it's a little like telling someone about how their foie gras is made as they're eating it. It doesn't stop you from continuing but a little of the enjoyment can be lost.

When you walk up to the lookout point above Tongue Bay (go in the afternoon when the sun is behind you) and see the view that's sold a million postcards and Whitsunday holidays you don't really think about how it was created. You just enjoy the moment. And that's really the point of coming to these islands.

Hire a boat and cruise around for a few days, with a few friends thrown in for added enjoyment. When you've had enough of wandering around to see what's what, park your boat about 200 metres off the delectable White Haven beach, turn on some soothing music, open a nice bottle of chilled white and lie back and enjoy the deep blue and parrot fish poo.

It's not just fish in the ocean that caught my eye!

India

India

A stint in India will beat the restlessness out of any living creature (Yann Martel, *Life of Pi*)

Holy Cow!

There are probably as many views on India as there are Indians.

'Your senses will be overwhelmed', 'you'll be appalled at the poverty', 'the pollution is horrendous', 'nothing works' and 'you're gonna get the shits' are just a few.

Well, we've landed in Kolkata at 1.30am and the immigration computer is down and now that the queues have grown to sweaty and chattering proportions there's a power cut. The case for 'nothing works' seems to be building.

We'll no doubt get to experience the other generalizations as we go but for now I'm more interested in a party. It's Diwali (also called Deepavali), the equivalent for many Hindus of Christmas and New Year rolled into one, where the Gods are honoured. Lord Shiva and Kali appear to be heading up the bill. Kali's home is Kolkata where legend has it that she was incarnated by Lord Shiva to vanquish demons and unsavoury characters that threatened the world. She's black (or blue) skinned, wild eyed with a bloody tongue stuck out and has a garland of demons' heads around her neck. Not the most attractive look but the locals love her all the same. Shiva's a good-looking chap with blue skin (something to do with swallowing the poisons of the world to save mankind). A pretty heady pair. There are images of them everywhere and even at 3am in the morning as we head through the city towards our hotel there are people in the streets enjoying the brightly painted and lit deity statues in their temporary street side altars. A pleasant surprise from the marauding hordes of beggars we'd been led to believe would meet us on arrival.

The hotel is a pleasant surprise too. Fairlawn is a bit of an institution with travellers and the press corps according to the manager. The place is actually an old home and for decades has been in the same family headed up by an English octogenarian matriarch. Upon waking the next day, the eclectic style of the place I thought I'd spotted through weary eyes when we arrived turned out to be real enough. It still feels like an old family house with family photos sharing as much if not more space with photos of the rich and famous who've stayed here. Don't expect 5-star splendour though as its bedrooms are, shall we say, functional and won't win any style awards. It's the delightfully eccentric feel and look to the place that will win your heart. You may even get allocated one of the rooms the likes of Patrick Swayze or Sting stayed in too. Not that I've tried any other hotel in Kolkata but if you're looking for an experience then you could do a lot worse than this.

Okay, so now it's time for an apology to China. Their standard of driving isn't even in the same league as these guys. One of our drivers proudly told us that if you can drive in India you can drive anywhere. I thought about this during the day's tour and responded later in the day by saying that if you drove like you did in India anywhere else in the world your life expectancy was probably fifteen minutes. Likewise, if you come here and drive like you would in your own country you'll also have fifteen minutes.

India notionally drives on the left but in reality drives wherever there's a space.

I noticed on the back of a taxi that it stated 'Obey the traffic rules'. The car taxis, by the way, are by and large an old British design from the 1950s that is still made to this day, in India, and is known as the Hindustan Ambassador. It's a wonderfully eccentric sight on the roads in bright green and yellow (or black and yellow depending on the city) and fits right in with the faded glory of a past empire that lingers in this old British Raj capital. There are rickshaw and tuk tuk 'taxis' too but you're best to stay with the cars as every vehicle has dents and pieces missing from them. A dent or piece missing from a car most likely means you aren't dented or don't have any pieces missing. I'm not sure you could say the same of the alternatives.

Our guide, Dev, was quick to point out with a chuckle that the instruction on the boot lid of the taxis basically meant red light stop, green light go, horn at all times. Horn when you turn, horn when you overtake, horn at anything in your way, horn if you haven't horned for the last five seconds. And after a few weeks of this driving madness I'd say she's right but I'd add a few additional comments.

Firstly, size matters. It's like a school playground you see. The knuckle dragging bully goes first. He's the truck or bus. Then it's cars followed by tuk tuks and so on down to those on bicycles and finally those on foot. You can try and fight against this hierarchy but if a bus wants the space you're in and you don't move you'll be visiting Lord Shiva and his buddies sooner than you think.

Now, we had some excellent drivers. They could all negotiate the potholes, unpredictable children, swivel-eyed suicidal dogs and other road vehicles with pin-point accuracy. On several occasions I was convinced there was no way we were going to miss another vehicle, or a stall holder selling chapatis, but we brushed past with barely an inch to spare without fail. The first time this happened I figured we'd escaped a collision through pure luck but after many hundreds of such encounters I put it down to the driver's skills which were uniquely attuned to the Indian way of driving. The drivers though would tell you that it's all pre-ordained and if it's their time to die then it's their time and nothing they do will change that.

Fatalism is big in India. But to an agnostic Englishman that's not the most comforting of thoughts when you're overtaking a bus, that's overtaking a tuk tuk, that's overtaking a schoolgirl on a bicycle and we're all going around a blind curve in the road!

When you're outside of the urban sprawl of the cities it's even worse as the country folk seem to think the road is for many things other than just getting you from A to B. They work here, their kids play here, they socialize and eat here, they take a piss here and if fate has decided it they may well die here too. Their complete lack of awareness of vehicles travelling inches from them makes it all the more incredible.

Actually I've not yet mentioned a special someone in this real-life game of chicken. The cow.

This farmyard animal is at the top of the pile. It's revered and is in fact a sacred animal to Hindus by virtue of its association with transporting the gods. As such you can't kill them and definitely can't eat them. Now in most countries you'll find them in fields either eating grass or pulling a plough. In India you find them all over the towns and cities freely wandering around the roads shitting everywhere, looking gormless and eating plastic bags. Not particularly good behaviour for a beast held in such high regard methinks but this is just one of a myriad of contradictions you'll find in this country.

India's a nuclear super power on the one hand and on the other Indians have a penchant for worshipping animals.

They have more millionaires than the US but the majority of the population are paupers (with a family that's frequently less well fed than their cow).

An effective method of 'traffic calming'.

It's the largest democracy (apparently) in the world but they can't get organized to provide the people with a clean water system, a sanitary sewerage system or even to get the faeces off the pavements.

And they just keep coming.

The Ganges is sacred too but industry dumps vast amounts of chemicals into it, humans dump dead bodies into it and animals just take a dump in it. I could write several pages just on contradictions but will leave this line of writing for now with a comment a head-wobbling guide made that may help your understanding.

'This is India.'

Deities and Death

Hinduism has, according to popular legend and myth, 360 million deities and gods. That's nearly one for every three Indians! It's all very complicated to a westerner but what I have figured out is that Brahma, Vishnu and Shiva are the top three. The Creator, The Preserver and The Destroyer. They then have wives and girlfriends (Vishnu, the old dog, has sixteen thousand) and of course children. Some of the kids are animals. I didn't really want to get into that (particularly as I'd already seen a temple with a depiction of a man shagging a camel) but there are a few you see a lot of. The missus likes Ganesh who's a chubby chap with an elephant head. He's got something to do with prosperity and good luck. You see him in cars a lot where good luck is probably most needed, along with good brakes. I quite like the monkey god, Hanuman, who looks like a cheeky scamp and up for a bit of fun. But it's all a bit complicated as I said and as I've not figured it out I won't dig myself a hole by trying to explain it any further, particularly as I used to get brain ache trying to understand the difference between Catholicism and Methodism. What I've described is sufficient for this story anyhow.

Now, we've made it to Varanasi which is one of the most sacred places in India for Hindus. Another one is Pushkar (home of Lord Brahma) but that's in the middle of nowhere and when we arrived I found out you're not allowed to eat meat or drink alcohol so on principle I'm not going to write about that.

So Varanasi then. Being such a sacred place it's not a surprise to see many deities and gods being worshipped. The Muslims also worship here and so do the Buddhists, but in much smaller numbers. It's the home of Lord Shiva and the main Hindu temple on this site has a world famous 'Shiva-ling' made from precious stones, gold and silver. A Shiva-ling is the depiction of Shiva's cock by the way. It's to celebrate the time he exposed himself. Well, if you've got it flaunt it!

It's a very ancient city that in a lot of ways doesn't feel as though it's come out of feudal times. When you're down at the steps of the Ghats, and stand shoulder to shoulder with women and men in their traditional saris and loincloths readying to immerse themselves in the holy river you could be in the sixteenth century. The ringtones of mobile phones (why do Indians have the volume turned up so high?) and adverts for the same tend to shatter the illusion though.

Varanasi is where all Hindus want to come to be cremated. Of the eighty-four ghats here several are burning ghats to accommodate this wish. There are several platforms in front of ornate Hindu temples, blackened with the wood smoke from below, that operate 24/7. We watched quietly from a row boat as the wood pyres were prepared, stoked and maintained. This last rite of a Hindu is only witnessed by male members of his or her family to avoid female emotions ruining the ascension to the next life apparently. It's a very moving experience that commands silence from onlookers, but for all the thoughts and feelings it stirs in you neither of us found it upsetting. The surprise is that you may well go away feeling a little more spiritual.

The bodies are wrapped in white linen, 'washed' in the Ganges and then placed on an individual pyre. India's lowest caste, the untouchables, manage the burning.

At the same time that evening, the Brahman priests start up their nightly 'Arti' ceremony praying to Lord Shiva. This is watched by thousands and the experience is quite powerful. Death and celebration go hand in hand in Varanasi.

On a dawn row boat ride the following morning it was heartwarming to see so many pilgrims' elation at reaching their holy place and cleansing themselves in the Ganges. I could only think that the 'cleansing' was psychological or spiritual as the river itself is filthy. Human and animal shit, rotting carrion and all manner of rubbish make it rather dangerous to your health but this doesn't seem to stop the locals. Not even a dead body of a man caught in a mooring rope only feet away from hundreds 'cleansing' themselves caught anyone's attention or concern. Except ours. Well, I suppose the poor bugger made it to his holy place at least, but probably not the way he would have planned it.

Surely they'll be dirtier when they get out than when they get in?

Baksheesh

Varanasi has also exposed us big time to beggars, hawkers, performers and the like. We'd seen these people in other places as well but here it was supercharged. With nightly Brahman performances on the ghats and a never-ending flow of tourists and devotees it's easy to see why so many seek easy money here. The stench from the streets is overwhelming and seems to be stuck to their every pore. Combine that with a dogged persistence that 'no' will at some point turn into 'yes' and your sensibilities become a little stretched even for a seasoned traveller.

This is the low rent end of a national business that everyone takes part in. No service is too small to ask for a tip or as the locals call it 'Baksheesh'. Sounds like a kebab but best not to put the worn and grubby ten rupee notes you'll need to keep handy anywhere near your mouth as they're probably the best way to experience Delhi belly in a hurry.

So I'm primed with my stack of Baksheesh money but know this is going to be a difficult affair as I'm a Brit and we just don't have a tipping culture. Neither does my adopted home so I always find it slightly uncomfortable when it comes time to provide a tip. I much prefer the approach of 'everything within the price' and if you feel a tip is warranted for outstanding service then it's at your discretion. Americans would argue that this removes your ability to reward for good service and penalize for bad but in my experience Stateside a rather large tip is expected whether they go out of their way to serve and help or whether they treat you like an inconvenience and spit in your soup.

And then you have the awful decision of who you don't give baksheesh to. You can get to the point where you think everyone wants it for everything, and the beggars are the worst.

'I've cut off my leg and poked out my eye so you'll feel sorry for me. Please give baksheesh.'

'Sir, please take notice of me banging my rented child's head on your car window. I'll stop if you give me baksheesh.'

'I've just farted sir, please give baksheesh!'

But you have to ignore these guys as if you once give to a beggar you'll attract the hordes waiting in the wings. A difficult slight for any westerner taught to be polite but a necessity here, we're told.

There are a few 'service' providers you can ignore too like the tour operator (but not the guide) or the receptionist of the hotel. The best rule is to give to the small guy. If he's a professional and speaks as an equal to you no need for baksheesh. If he's licking your boots within five seconds of meeting you you'd better get counting.

India generally treats a tourist as a walking wallet and so politeness abounds from everyone. This may well change after you've tipped though depending on whether they think they've been justly rewarded. The majority will smile and not look at the amount you've pressed into their palm preferring good manners to being rude. But don't be surprised if at some point someone looks at you as though you've just put a turd into their hand. There's no such thing as too much as far as the receiver is concerned and a little psychological pressure to extract more may be rude but makes good business sense.

Now look, just don't buy into it. Give what you feel is fair, offer thanks with a smile and leave with a confident gait. I've not found anyone who's thrown it back in my face or verbally assaulted me so maybe I've got it about right. Or is it that I'm just giving them too much to start with?

Maharajas, Mughals and a guy called Sid

We came to India (my wife reluctantly) to do a number of things, but primarily to experience the remnants of past empires from the Mughals to the Maharajahs and also to see the temples and mausoleums built in the name of Hinduism, Islam and Buddhism. We also wanted to see the tigers but the poachers seem to have put paid to that.

There was no disappointment with the forts and palaces of Rajasthan though and the rather risqué Hindu temples in Khajaraho proved to be a crowd pleaser too. The stone carvings covering the temples here have some seriously erotic Karma Sutra poses that would negate the local youth having to ask their parents about the birds and the bees. There were quite a few red faces pushed to zoom lenses that may not have been from sunburn.

The most famous of all Indian buildings also proved to be a joy. The Taj Mahal is quite simply an architectural gem and rightly considered one of the man-made wonders of the world. I always thought it was painted but the intricate designs that adorn the white marble walls are in fact inlaid stone ranging from various coloured marble to jasper, malachite, lapis lazuli and onyx. Shah Jehan must have really had it bad for his favourite wife Mumtaz Mahal to have spent twenty-two years and today's equivalent of several billion dollars to build this. Just goes to prove that quality will last far longer than the memory of the price.

The guides we used throughout our trip generally give you a picture of religious tolerance across the country. This can be frequently proven untrue throughout history (including very recent bombings and hijackings) but the architecture of many of India's great rulers does add credence to this being a worthy goal at least. Hindu and Muslim symbology is found intertwined everywhere. They may have a small difference of 359,999,999 gods they worship but that doesn't seem to be a barrier to creating art and architecture that celebrates both.

India is also the birthplace of that most famous of non-religions, Buddhism.

It all started with a guy called Siddhartha. He was a real man and he was also a prince. Born 563 BC into a Hindu royal family he wasn't happy with his lot so went off in search of enlightenment. He found it under a ficus tree in Boghgaya and then gave his first sermon in Sarnath. We went to have a look but there's not a lot left since the Mughals ransacked the place some time ago. They do still have a tree though and a group of benefactors have erected a new temple but it's not on the grand scale or level of exuberance you'll find in the Hindu and Islamic piles dotted across the country. I somehow think Sid would have liked it that way.

Threesomes are so passé.

A caste of thousands

Indians love cricket. They play it all over the place, sometimes even when they haven't got stumps or a ball. There's even a TV channel where the only thing you can watch is cricket. I know this as one night I was forced to watch it in our hotel (being the only English- speaking programme on offer) as they didn't have a bar and the missus had already gone to sleep. It's a leftover from the British and just like bureaucracy the Indians are looking to perfect it. Now the reason I mention this game is because I think it's a good metaphor for India.

Its rules are complicated, it's not always obvious what's going on, you can go to sleep through large chunks of it and it's all likely to stop every time it rains.

But just like every other sport the players all have a role. And so it is with Indian society.

What I'm describing here is an ancient system for determining your place in the grand scheme of things. As Hindus believe in reincarnation it's a rather important system because if you lead a pious life you may well be rewarded with a step up the ladder the next time you're born. Dying first seems like a fairly harsh way to get a promotion to me but while you're alive there have historically been very limited options open to Indians and a whole host of roadblocks in your way, not least of which is your family.

The caste system is officially defunct these days according to the constitution but try telling that to your mother. You see, the vast majority of weddings are still arranged and no self respecting mother would want little Sanjay or Shanti to marry down so you can easily find yourself stuck in caste limbo with no one accepting you moving up.

If you're born into the bottom caste, the untouchables, no one will be touching you apart from the dead and the scared, both of whose money you'll be taking. If you're born into the top caste of Brahman you'll basically be doing what you want or what makes most money, even though you're supposed to be a priest. And if you're somewhere in between you'll be largely stereotyped based on what your ancestors did.

But in these days when parts of India are modernizing it seems there are ways in which you can shake off the shackles of your ancestors and live the democratic dream. You could be adept at business or you may have the luck to get properly educated and become a doctor, in each case wealth may well come your way.

If you're a pretty girl with big boobs or a swarthy guy with big sunglasses though you may well have the golden ticket and make it all the way to the cast(e) of Bollywood.

So it is that we've come to the end of our Indian odyssey and find ourselves in Mumbai. Home of sitar-backed synchronized dancing, identi-kit stars and starlets and India's financial system. It's also where the Brits went home from, after their reign ended. There's still a rather nice gateway here on the waterfront, built for a king's arrival but which also marks the occasion of an empire leaving.

Out of all the places we've visited this one is where the rich aspire to live. Right next door to millions of the poor. It didn't catch either of our imaginations though and with a skyline of soulless concrete and pollution it isn't somewhere we'll come back to.

It was however, the first place in India we'd been to where we were able to find a great restaurant that didn't sell curry. I even had a gourmet beefburger! Oh, heaven. It turned out to be buffalo due to the 'free pass – do not go to the abattoir' card the cows possess (another meat to add to my growing list) but when it tasted that good, the exact point of origin on the bovine evolutionary tree wasn't of any great concern to me.

A glass of wine in a comfortable café atmosphere was also a chance to reflect on this country.

The people are generally friendly and accommodating and always smiling. Even those with no money, or no legs, seem to be smiling. And everyone's an entrepreneur. Whether they're six or sixty they've got an angle to push. Such optimism and ambition is a wonderful thing, often in the face of grinding poverty and overwhelming odds against success.

You get the impression that Indians truly love India and may even show a little pity for you that you're not an Indian too.

Now it's true that if you ask a question you could get three different answers from the same person or from three different persons. I've had to re-write this chapter several times after receiving misleading or inaccurate information from those who feel it's better to give an answer, any answer, whether it's right or wrong than admit failure to know. This is when I also realized that the head bobbing when answering can mean yes, no or maybe. Sometimes, all three at the same time. I'm obviously not going to get to understand this place in the short time we've been here but it's been a very colourful experience to rival the rainbow of saris and tribal dress on display every day in every state just the same.

We've taken trains, cars, tuk tuks, elephants and camels from Kolkata on the east coast to Jaisalmer close to the Pakistan border and then a plane to get to Mumbai on the western seaboard. The sights are truly stunning one minute and appalling the next, but never forgettable.

You'll get the shits no matter how hard you try not to swallow shower water or how often you clean your hands and it probably won't be from the food (which was generally great). It'll be a mystery but in a country where you can never stay clean for very long, get it you will.

You'll also never really feel relaxed which is weird in a country that invented yoga, meditation and several non-violent religions. Nearly dying horribly in a car because a cow decides to walk in front of you for no reason other than it's maybe spotted a plastic bag it likes on the other side of the road is just one reason you'll find it difficult to nod off. The never-ending street noise and chatter of conversation will get under your skin as well and together with the smell of spice impregnate every pore.

So come here with an open mind, a thick skin and a sense of humour as you'll be needing all within minutes of landing.

And I guess that just leaves the question, do I like India?

Well yes.

No.

Maybe.

Southern Africa

Mozambique

How to forget work

I can't tell you how much we've been looking forward to the second of our beach breaks on this round the world trip. Kicking back and doing sod all for a week is going to be such a wonderful way to relax, contemplate what we've been up to so far and daydream about what's to come. And so it is that we've made it to Mozambique.

I've always thought it was a wonderfully exotic sounding place and it turns out it lives up to this image. The Portuguese were here long enough to have the locals speaking their lingo but not long enough to have them making fortified wine, or any wine, but that's okay as their neighbour is South Africa and they have lots.

It's not the richest of African nations and isn't really famous for anything I can immediately think of but we've come here because they apparently have whale sharks swimming past all year round.

Now, we've seen whales already in New Zealand and we could have gone to see more of various types off of Western Australia but generally the tour operators aren't allowed to let you in the water with them.

Something to do with being crushed by a tonne and a half of pectoral fin or making the whales scared. So you pay a bloody fortune to, if you're lucky, see the back and flukes of a whale preceded and followed by massive expanses of ocean and a few seagulls. But all is different with the whale shark. You can get in the water with them.

As they don't have teeth they won't bite you and because they move really slowly they're great for taking photos of and are unlikely to crush you with a tale swipe that you haven't already seen coming for the past ten seconds.

But this is where things really get interesting because when you go to see whale sharks in Mozambique you don't go in a touristy catamaran with onboard TV, comfy seats and compulsory lifejackets, oh no. You go on what I can only describe as a special forces speed boat. I've not been in a special forces speed boat but I've seen a few on the TV and this looks like that, except it's white.

It's essentially a rubber dinghy with a hard hull and two bloody great four-stroke outboards strapped to the back. Oh yes, and no seats. The driver stands at the front next to what looks like a lectern, with a throttle and a steering wheel, and everyone else sits on the two sides of the rubber dinghy.

This is starting to get really interesting!

So first there's a briefing which is more about how not to touch the whale sharks or set off a camera flash six inches from their faces and very little about this fearsome-looking boat we'll be riding. Then they put you into a Land Rover, with the top cut off, that looks like it's been in a few civil wars and drive you across a beautiful beige sand beach to the water's edge.

Here all ten of us are required to help get the boat into deeper water. The driver of the Land Rover tells us to jump off and go and wait in the surf, keeping our feet away from the trailer wheels and our faces away from the hull that is about to be hurled at us. He then reverses the boat, on its trailer at speed into the ocean jettisoning it off its trailer, and shouts for us to catch it. Captain Dumbo (I'd swear that's how he pronounced it even if it wasn't actually what he meant) then asks the boys on the left to turn the boat into the ocean and scramble on before we're dragged underneath and drowned.

By this time there are a few faces thinking this can't be legal but I'm loving it. It then gets dramatically more fun. When you sit down on the inflated rubber side of the boat you're told to put your feet in the footstraps screwed to the floor and hold on. Footstraps!

When Captain Dumbo floors the twin Suzuki motors you find out why. We're flung backwards and within seconds are at 30 degrees nose up as we take off over the incoming waves. I felt like we were in *Bondi Rescue* or a Jean-Claude Van Damme movie or something. And we hadn't even seen a whale shark yet.

From this vantage point you get to see the fairly rugged, very sparsely populated coastline of Inhambane for beautiful mile after mile of deserted fine sand beaches.

We'd taken a quad bike tour the previous day and rode along the same stretch and it was wonderful. Just like with the boat they didn't have much to tell you apart from get on, start it up and squeeze the throttle. They only mentioned the helmets we could have used when we got back.

We rode on dirt roads, through wood-hut villages

and along clifftops sometimes at what seemed like serious speed. No one crashed, no one cared how fast we drove and everyone had huge dusty grins on their faces.

Looking around the boat the same was true today. The initial shock of westerners encountering a trip that didn't involve helmets and an hour of safety lecturing, followed by a usually flaccid experience, had now converted to smiles.

When we found a whale shark or two to swim with this just made the day perfect. I urge anyone who can swim to do this. Preferably in Mozambique because then you'll also get the ride of your life, but find somewhere you can go and see these gorgeous creatures. Actually being in the water with such an enormous, graceful and gentle creature is really one of the best things you can do with a day of your life.

So, time to head back. Amazingly the thrills weren't yet over. We'd grown accustomed to the manic speed of the boat and hanging on for dear life so that wasn't going to give us an extra adrenalin shot. What was would be the next 500 metres. We'd stopped about this distance away from the beach and were told that we'd need to hang on to the boat even harder and make sure our feet were fully braced within the footstraps because we were going to race at high speed at the shore to make sure we'd successfully 'beach the boat'. This immediately had everyone staring at each other and me remembering lying on a beach once in Crete and a local jockstrap doing the very same manoeuvre on a jetski. The jetski stopped abruptly after contacting the sand and the Greek budgie smuggler flew over the handlebars, legs akimbo and landed flat on his back. He quickly got up to look at the machine with an air of 'I think there must be something wrong with my jetski' but had obviously put trying to look cool ahead of physics.

Were we about to make the same mistake and become the butt of someone else's anecdote?

We're now only 100 metres away and are crashing through the surf and the beach is coming at us at a rate of knots. Within a split second the engines are cut, the bow hits the sand and we all jolt forwards as we stop, but amazingly don't get catapulted over the captain who's standing at the wheel grinning.

You'd think this would be it but then of course gravity takes over and the V-shaped hull of the boat has to make a decision if it's going to heel left or right. I then find myself an extra metre in the air. The girls on board had made a few squeaks during the last thirty seconds (and I'd swear so did a couple of the boys) but now all is silent as we gingerly extricate ourselves from one of the most fun watercraft I've ever had a go on.

This trip and the one on the quad bikes sums up quite nicely one of the two reasons you should come to Mozambique. They treat you like intelligent adults and assume you know something about what you're planning on signing up for and not like an imbecile who's likely to hurt himself getting out of bed. I like this a lot.

Most places you'll ever go to will dumb down the experience to accommodate greater numbers so they can, in theory, make more money or because health and safety laws insist you must wear 10kg of protective clothing. This is the bane of most 'exciting experiences' you'll find in the 'civilized' world. But in Mozambique they say 'Pah!'

They really do give value for money (the whale shark

safari was about one-fifth of the cost of several whale 'watching' trips we've been on!!) and you'd be hard pressed to add much excitement to the standard package, I can tell you.

The other reason you should come here is because not many other people are at the moment. I guess memories of the now long past civil war are still in people's minds. This means development is minimal, the locals haven't yet resorted to turning their children into trinket salesmen at the age of six and you'll get to enjoy very reasonable food and alcohol prices.

We stayed in a place with water villas on stilts over a tidal inlet. It's all very calm and relaxed and the local staff couldn't have been nicer. They also had some wonderful seafood that the missus took no time in demolishing most days and quite one of the best steaks I've ever tasted. Paying significantly less than you would anywhere in Asia (why is it so expensive?!) for a decent bottle of wine to accompany you on your deck watching the sunset also didn't hurt.

And it was on this deck, sitting peacefully with the sound of the ocean lapping lazily below and the sun setting in the distance that it slowly dawned on me that I had finally dispelled all idea of work from my head.

So there you are. Mozambique. A great place to forget work.

South Africa

Carcharodon carcharias

For the first half of my life South Africa wasn't somewhere you would have associated with a holiday. It was in fact a pariah state probably on the same list of undesirables as Libya in the 1980s, albeit for a different reason. Up until Mandela was freed in 1990 and for a few years subsequently until he became president it was in all likelihood the world's largest 'old boy's club'. A playground for the white Afrikaans where rugby and beer were their happy drugs and the indigenous population were largely in the way.

These days the black and white division enforced by apartheid has been replaced by a division of 'haves and have-nots' bringing it into line with the rest of the democratic world. The general feeling you get on the street though is that the haves are generally white and the have-nots generally black. Time and good governance will hopefully see this balancing a little more in years to come.

Well, here we are. We've come to the Western Cape as this to me is the South Africa I want to see. Yes, there's lots of game reserves (probably the most famous being Kruger) but we're going to be spending three weeks on an expedition through Namibia and Botswana so no point in doubling up.

What you can't see in Namibia and Botswana is the glorious Cape Peninsula.

Cape Town and the Cape Peninsula is, we've discovered, a great place to while away a week or so. It's a small part of the country for sure but probably one of the nicest.

Before the Suez Canal was opened the Cape of Good Hope was the only way to India and the Far East by sea. Not surprisingly then, the Dutch and the British (and quite a few other states) had a keen interest in it. It's cosmopolitan to this day and you can easily find foods to suit all palates, but no matter what you eat you must try a Cape Malay Curry and the local seafood. With wine from just up the road in Stellenbosch and Franschhoek, at a very reasonable price, you could easily be forgiven for spending most days on the beach, around the pool or on the harbour front eating, drinking and slowly slipping into a happy torpor for days at a time. We did just that but also managed to slap ourselves awake to see a little more than the playground of the blonde and the beautiful.

A drive down to the tip of the Peninsula is something you should definitely do if you come here. Take the Chapman Peak Drive from Hout Bay along the Atlantic Ocean. It's a scenic gem, not to mention a driver's wet dream. You hug the cliff face with hills and mountains above as you wind around the natural undulations of the coast. Popping out at the southern end of this drive you're greeted by a large crescent-moon shaped bay below. Kommetjie isn't a rich town but it has one hell of a beautiful white sand beach that's lapped by a sea of pure aquamarine and turquoise.

This whole Peninsula is effectively a national Park, save the low-lying land generally on the ocean front. Mother Nature's design and man's planning at its best. Ocean views for all the residents and mountain parks for all the animals. Table Mountain National Park goes all the way from Cape Town right down to the Cape of Good Hope. Without a doubt the namesake of the park is the most spectacular peak to look at and look down from but the rest of the peaks in this range are no less dramatic. The whole thing gives you the feeling it was drawn by a five-year-old with crayons. Improbably pointy witches' hats next to roller-coaster ride undulations next to sheer cliffs and craggy outcrops and of course the flat top of a table (frequently draped with a tablecloth of rolling white clouds).

Cape Point (the most southerly point on the Peninsula) and the Cape of Good Hope sit about a mile apart, like two points of a snake's forked tongue. On the calm and sunny day we'd picked (not at all forboding as this seafarers' nightmare has generally been portrayed through history) we were treated to a light breeze, miniature elephants, baboons and ostriches. And of course a view towards Antarctica. The ostriches were grazing at the roadside a hundred metres from the sign that marks the Cape of Good Hope. An unusual sight on a rocky coast at the southern tip of a continent. The sign itself had busloads of Koreans and Germans jockeying to get a photo with it before quickly scrambling back in to their air-conditioned seats. A few baboons were sitting sentinel on various high points along the path that takes you up to Cape Point lighthouse. You could smell them before you saw them and with one in particular you could hear him before you could smell him. He was emitting a sort of bark reminiscent of a dog that's just been kicked in the nuts. Seemed a good idea to give him a wide berth.

I sort of fibbed about the miniature elephants. There are rock hyrax (or dassies as the locals call them) all over the peninsula. They look more like a guinea pig than an elephant but apparently they're a distant cousin. Cute and curious little things.

We had to go further south towards Cape Aguhlus on the most southerly point of Africa to see the creature I'd really come here for though. The great white shark. And this is where I have to backtrack a little on my Mozambique rant about safety gear. Getting into the ocean with four to five metres of finely tuned predator is best done with some metal between you.

The boat itself was designed specifically for shark cage diving. It was pretty big which was a relief as I'm old enough to remember *Jaws*, that most famous of shark movies, and a startled Roy Scheider dropping back to the deck after just coming face to face with several rows of razor-sharp teeth in a gaping mouth and uttering the immortal line 'I think we're gonna need a bigger boat!'

The day we power out of the harbour it's a little choppy. Our shark boat has indeed been well designed though, as it's just cutting through the squally conditions like a knife through butter. Not a single person is feeling seasick although there are a few looking a little apprehensive. Can't think why.

We were only ten minutes into the trip when we saw the first. Our jovial captain had been so confident at the briefing that this would happen he'd even gone as far as saying we'd see at least eight different sharks today. By the end of the day we'd actually seen thirteen. Thirteen great whites, that had passed within feet of our faces more than one hundred times in total. And when I say within feet of our faces I do actually mean that literally.

You put on a wet suit and a mask and drop into a cage that's tied to the side of the boat. Making sure you keep your fingers and toes inside the cage (important this!) you then wait for the beasties to arrive. This process is speeded up with the crew chumming the water with foul smelling fish parts and blood. When a shark is spotted they then use a couple of added incentives for the sharks to stick around. Nope, not seven tourists in a cage strapped to the side of a boat, we were reassured, but lures.

One is a two-dimensional silhouette of a seal pup made from wood and rubber. I'd had a good look at this before we were in the water and it had a lot of teeth marks in it. The other was half a mullet and a tuna's head. Both turned out to be highly effective.

So, here we are bobbing around in rather chilly water at the southern end of the Atlantic Ocean trying to meet face to face with a great white shark. On reflection, as the cold seawater seeped into my wetsuit and the waves rolled over my head, this may not have been my best macho decision. I was excited on the boat and a little cautious getting into the cage and was now alternating between wondering how long it takes to get hypothermia and if the cage was made of thick enough wire but I still didn't know what I'd feel when the first shark arrived. Fear? I was about to find out.

A male made a first pass to see what was what. He was probably three metres from the cage. When he came back he virtually brushed it. On the third pass he definitely seemed to be looking at me. A great white's eyes are steely pools of grey that don't seem to move but just like with a portrait, you know when they're looking at you.

On his fourth pass he was swimming with a little more urgency and on his fifth he came up from the deep and made a lunge for the fish lure. A crew hand quickly pulled it through the water to keep the shark interested in his prey. He was pulling it straight towards the boat, and towards the cage. The shark's jaws opened to bite and as the lure was yanked out of the water there was little distance between a pearly white set of gnashers attached to half a tonne of shark and me. Gulp.

It seemed a collision was imminent but at the last second he twisted left and darted away leaving my mind a little blurry on detail for the next few seconds. Coming up for air I couldn't help grinning and swearing at the same time. I now knew the rest of the day was really going to be one to remember. Pure exhilaration was what I was feeling. A slightly startled exhilaration initially, but exhilaration nonetheless. Such a beautiful creature with so much grace and presence. Coming face to face with one like this could only leave you in awe, I could now confirm. Speaking to my fellow divers over a warm drink between cage time everyone was the same. No one felt fear.

The time afforded to us with the great whites was lengthy but still not enough. Everyone on board spent at least forty minutes (in two twenty-minute sessions) in the water and for every minute there was at least one shark to see.

They were flying in from the right and from the left. They would come straight at us and sometimes forget to turn. Once, when I wasn't in the cage, a shark forgot to turn or maybe was so busy chasing the lure he ran out of time to turn but either way he hit the cage head on. Everyone on board shrieked or gasped. This was a YouTube moment.

Everyone in the cage fair shit themselves.

After they had composed themselves and got out they did say it was difficult to take in when it happened but were pleased it was a story they were able to take home. I wasn't sure anyone would believe them as it sounds a bit like one of those fishing trips with 'the one that got away' but it did happen. The missus captured it on video from the deck of the boat and now it's on the web.

Four hours on a rocking boat in a stiff breeze off the southern end of Africa passed in what seemed like moments. A truly wonderful memory to mark our third 'bottom of the world' experience.

One of nature's most awesome creations. Best seen from an over-engineered cage.

Namibia

Dali would have loved this place

Sand. Lots and lots of sand.

That's the overwhelming memory you have of this former German colony. They apparently have lots of diamonds too but after getting married last year and paying a king's ransom for a ring and matching baubles I figured best not to tempt my better half with that.

So we stuck with sand.

We went to Sossusvlei in the Namib desert to see the other-worldly sand dunes. The wind comes alternately from the Atlantic Ocean and the Kalahari desert and means they only grow in size and don't move, unlike the dunes in, say, the Sahara. It also means that every so often a new dune is formed between two existing ones which blocks off the ability for life to sustain itself on the Atlantic side. Over hundreds of years this creates a Salvador Dali-esque scene of dried up limestone pools, cracked by the heat of the day, with the dead husks of acacia trees eerily black against a backdrop of red sand and blue sky. The only thing missing is the melted clocks.

We also got to find out about a lot of the animal life here. Yep, this death trap of a place has lots going on, albeit quite surreal. And the names are even weirder.

There are sand diving lizards. Yes, they do actually dive into the sand which is rather humorous. Our guide caught one and then got it to dive for us. Then there are baboon spiders. I'm not sure how they got their name as they live in the sand and we haven't seen any baboons but they're here, if like our guide you know where to look. And my personal favourite, headstand beetles. And yes, they do stand on their heads. With their arses in the air they catch the morning dew on their large derrières and let it trickle down to their mouths. I'm not convinced this is either hygienic or the easiest solution to the problem but the guide said that's what they did and I love the craziness of it.

And to top it all we had a bushman showing us around from a tribe that clicks. You may never have heard this but it's a very unique way of talking. Sentences and key words start with a clicking sound made by pushing your tongue to the roof of your mouth and then pulling it down hard. He loved dancing and hated shoes.

I think Salvador would have liked it here.

And more sand

We also went to Swakopmund which is a strange town with seemingly no one, but lots of houses. Outside of the hotel we saw probably only thirty people in the whole two days we were here. No one seems to walk the streets (except us), there are very few cars on the road and the restaurants weren't full. Where is everyone?

It was sand here again that took our interest, heading out with an adventure company to quad bike the sand dunes and then take a board and slide down a monster of a dune. It's called sandboarding and consists of no more than you lying on a flexible woodfibre board, holding up the front edge and getting off when you get to the bottom.

The eight or so seconds in between as you plummet head first down the dune though are something else. They reckon you can get up to 80 km/h on one of these things. I wouldn't doubt it having done it. It gives you a real rush. 80 km/h with no seat belt, or come to that no seat. No safety gear and no steering. Good job we're not in the West else they'd have banned it and locked up the people responsible. In fact, it only came with one drawback (assuming you don't include having your shorts filled with sand a drawback). Once you're at the bottom you've got to walk back up. Have you ever tried running on soft hot sand on a beach? Now, take that feeling and the effort involved and apply it to a mountain of sand over 200 metres high. By the time you've scrambled up 300 metres of sand your legs are quivering like a dog who's found a vicar's leg. Yep, I said 300 metres, because for every step you take forwards you sink into the sand and only make a fraction of that step in progress. And on some of the really steep bits you'd better try and run else you'll get nowhere.

But just like a child high on fun, when you reach the top and start accelerating downhill again you forget the pain. For oh, I don't know, maybe thirty seconds.

We managed it five times before even my optimistic nature (more likely my 40-year-old legs and lungs I hear you say) decided it was time to get back on the bikes and ride a few more dunes before heading home.

So, sandboarding. It would be a perfect pastime, with one modification.

A ski-lift.

Game viewing consists of two groups of people. Some shouting 'there there' and the other shouting 'where where'.
(Rose Rigden's Wildside.)

The temperature here is depressingly and consistently hot. This wouldn't be so bad if the vehicle we were in had air-conditioning or something resembling a suspension system to cope with the gravel and dirt tracks that pass as roads. I was starting to smell like a baboon's armpit and had lost all feeling in my legs too.

Even my coccyx could forgive the bastard child of a truck and a bus we'd been riding in for the last 3000km though upon arrival in Etosha National Park. The rooms were lovely, they had a shop that sold Magnums and there was an animal watering hole only fifty metres from our front door. This watering hole we later found to be chock-a-block full of animals just at that time of day when a nice gin and tonic seems like a good idea. And you could have one. Right next to the watering hole.

But before all of that we'd been on a game drive and seen everything from springbok, oryx and kudu to giraffe, zebra, lions eating a zebra, elephants and rhinoceros. A male lion even walked right in front of us. He was a big brute. Completely in control of the terrain for miles and his presence just simply electrified the prey animals. It did a pretty good job of waking us up too.

To see any of these animals in the wild is to really

experience the true glory of nature. But when you see something as rare as a black rhino you know you've witnessed something special. We saw three in one day which apparently is very very lucky.

We saw white rhinos too, which are less rare, but to the untrained eye look the same as the blacks. Neither is black or white as the names suggest but more of a battleship grey colour. Their mouths are the easiest way to tell them apart. The black has a downward hooked upper lip for pulling foliage from bushes and the white has a flat fat-lipped mouth like Mick Jagger.

These guys, plus most things with a pulse, had got everyone on our overlanding expedition clamouring for a better look. Overlanding, by the way, is the term Southern Africans use for driving across large distances generally through sparsely populated areas. Not easy to do in a VW hatchback so they have specialist vehicles. Ours is called Pavarotti. For no good reason anyone can explain. It's basically a standard truck cab and chassis with a custom seating area plonked where the cargo area would normally be. Beneath and at the back of the seating area are storage spaces for a rudimentary kitchen, chairs, food, drink and luggage. It'll take up to twenty-four passengers but we're just twelve so have the chance to lounge around on board a little, which as it turns out is necessary wiggle room as we bump, vibrate and bounce our way from Cape Town through Namibia and Botswana to Zimbabwe. Over 5400km in all.

The animals were a major reason for us to be on this trip and so far we're not disappointed. Leopards are proving rather elusive but almost everything else has been sighted. And mostly right next to the tracks we're travelling on. Now, I'm not complaining but why is that? There are literally thousands of kilometres of savannah, acacia bush and semi-desert out here and the animals are right next to the roads. There aren't any fences, there's no more food by the roads we can see (except the animals themselves) and there's precious little to hide behind for hours on end. Yet here they are. Are humans considered a safety zone by the locals? Or perhaps it's the animals who've come to see us in our cages.

Botswana

What a way to go ...

I've never really thought much about death historically. Even though I've spent a greater portion of my working life on planes than most pilots it never enters my mind that we might crash.

Well, that's not strictly true as I did once nearly soil myself when an engine fell off as the plane I was on was speeding down the runway for take-off. I used to parachute too and had a couple of chute malfunctions which is also a good way of curing constipation. And now I come to think of it I also remember, from my teens, coming to a sliding halt in my car rather late, in the snow, and having a religious moment. But the point I'm getting at is that I've never really thought about it much. We all know it's going to happen but unless you're an Al-Qaeda suicide bomber we don't know when or how.

In the odd moment I give it consideration, I find it comforting to think that shuffling off my mortal coil whilst asleep, or riding a vestal virgin, would be about as good as it gets but having come to Botswana there's maybe a third option to consider.

We've flown into the Okavango Delta which is a rather beautiful part of Africa. On the face of it you get the impression this place is really a folly of nature because it seems like a mistake. You see, the namesake river took a wrong turn on its way to the sea and ended up in the semi-desert lands of Botswana. The delta is exactly what you'd expect to find at the mouth of a river that finds itself on very flat land just before it hits the sea. Except there's no sea.

So here we are, effectively in the middle of a desert and looking at a vast wetland. And there's no river flowing out. It just spreads out to form the delta and then sinks into the ground. There are waterways amongst the trees, islands, hippo grass and papyrus reeds. They're made by hippopotamus and elephant apparently and make for lovely canals to take a boat ride on. Devoid of telephones and the internet, not to mention humans (except your fellow travellers and the hired help of course) it really is a place you could come to to get away from it all for a while.

So here I am trekking through the Okavango Delta in search of big game with nothing more than a camera and a good dose of optimism when a fellow trekker says, 'I think it would be really something to meet your death by being eaten by a wild animal. What a way to go, hey?!'

She had a hint of cheeky questioning to the comment and a mischievous smile so my brain switched on. I thought about it for a few minutes and had to say she had at least a pub point. You know, one of those subjects you talk about in the pub when you've had a few.

It would certainly look good on your curriculum vitae of life. I mean, would you rather spend your last moments in a hospital bed wetting yourself and dribbling or getting your head ripped off by a wild animal? The latter would certainly give you more dignity and the family an anecdote that would last for generations. So we humoured ourselves a little longer.

I'm not sure you'd want to die at the hands of all the wildlife we were encountering though. I mean, death by zebra doesn't sound very manly. Nor does death by gnu for that matter. And most definitely not warthog, which is essentially a pig with tusks. There were lots of these in and around our camp, which by the way was wonderful. We stayed in tents but ones which were on wooden platforms with balconies, had proper beds and porcelain toilets and sinks and a proper shower. The shower was outdoors and I can tell you that standing naked in the breeze outdoors under a cool stream of water in the hot air has to rank up there with receiving a giant birthday cake full of naked girls.

Cape buffalo or giraffe don't really cut it either and having been up close and personal with a pod of hippos I think that would be more a comical than impressive way to pop your clogs. It's something to do with their piggy eyes. Anything with an arse that big can't be macho either.

But would you believe they're the number one animal killer of humans in Africa? This isn't so hard to believe when you see how fast they can move (in or out of water) and just how big their jaws and tusks are. Why has a vegetarian got such big teeth by the way?

The fact that they're all a little pissy too just adds to the likelihood that timing your passing manoeuvre wrong may result in your boat ending up upside down with a hippo's arse in your face or your arse in his face. I'm not sure what would be worse.

We were out on a boat ride one day and saw plenty in the water. When they blocked the waterways we were riding along you'd have thought that their fearsome reputation would have us retreating the way we came but the guide had other ideas and essentially accelerated full throttle straight at them. I'm writing this so obviously I survived but it didn't seem such a clever idea at the time. They didn't look too happy when they came back up again after ducking underwater out of the way.

It was rather exciting though.

The boats are made of aluminium as hippos find this harder to chew through but a week earlier this didn't stop one ripping the bow off a boat that got too close. The two Japanese tourists and their guide (who was called Luckson by the way; what an apt name) managed to escape but the boat hasn't yet been dragged off the river bed. Gulp. Pleased we didn't meet these most unlikely killers out on our walk, especially as Luckson was again the guide.

Anyway, we decided that dying at the jaws or hooves of a vegetarian of any kind would be right out of order. An encounter with a bull elephant had us considering whether an exemption should be made but we were quickly settling on crocodiles or big cats. The problem with a crocodile though is that they drown you. That doesn't sound quick enough or dignified enough. So, how about a pride of female lions jumping on you and crushing your skull or maybe a surprise attack from a leopard who'll snap your neck like a chicken?

She thought leopard and given the fact seeing one is a real rarity this would fit the bill nicely as an impressive way to go. In fact, we still haven't seen one, only the remains of an impala that had been dragged up a tree by one for safekeeping from the hyenas lurking in the bushes.

Anyway, I couldn't decide mainly because I really don't want to die today, or any day soon.

Back at the tent I was having a shower after the heat of the walk and smiling at the thought of how vulnerable we were out here – no fences, no weapons and no way out without a boat and a Cessna – when something else dawned on me. Looking up I noticed that the tree we were tented under was a sausage tree. Yes, there really is such a thing but there isn't an ounce of pork involved. The sausages are elongated tree fruits. Each can weigh up to seven kilos and when they are ripe enough they fall to the ground. Now seven kilos dropping thirty feet will make quite a dent in whatever it hits whether that be the ground, or your head. There's a sausage swinging directly over the shower.

Death by sausage. Oh good grief. What a way to go.

The Okavango Delta is a great place to relax. As long as you're nowhere near a hippo or a sausage tree.

Zimbabwe

...scenes so lovely that they must have been gazed upon by angels in their flight. (David Livingstone, 1855)

I nearly went to live in Rhodesia when I was twelve. Dad had been offered a job to help run the Wanke power station (can't tell you how many sniggers that elicited from my brothers and me) but for reasons unknown to us we finally never went to what is now known as Zimbabwe. This may have been a fortuitous decision on behalf of my family given the country's more recent history, and very recent economic and currency collapse, but a trip to Southern Africa just wouldn't have been complete without a few days seeing a small part of this ex-Commonwealth state.

Our driver/guide and cook over the last three weeks travelling up from Cape Town were Zimbabweans and they were wonderful. Not just as human company but as professionals in their given jobs. Gertie could rustle up lunch in the middle of a desert that would have you asking for seconds, and eagerly awaiting dinner time, with seemingly effortless efficiency . And Johannes could drive for hours on end whilst we nodded off and then cheerily take you on an excursion without a hint of lethargy.

Once he even managed to save us from a vehicle malfunction with a speed that a cheetah would have been proud of. I'd asked if we could stop to photograph what was the most stunning sunset I've ever seen (and I've seen a few). The sky had turned to molten-lava red with splashes of yellow and orange as the sun started to disappear behind the Namib desert and the Atlantic Ocean in the distance. Eye-wateringly beautiful.

We heard what sounded like a fire extinguisher going off behind us approximately where we'd left Pavarotti and turned round to see Johannes diving underneath to put out a fire. I guess stopping had been a good idea at that particular moment, but the point is that our new Zimbabwean comrades were a resourceful pair.

When we got to Zimbabwe we found all the locals likeable and capable of looking after themselves too. These are good traits generally in any person but in recent months in Zimbabwe it is a necessity as the country's inept leadership has seen Zimbabwe free-falling into hyperinflation. You'd have been hard pressed to buy a loaf of bread with a trillion dollars and by the time you'd got your weekly wages they'd be worth half as much as they were the previous week. I remember studying hyperinflation at university and simplistically it creates a downward spiral of no confidence in your currency that results in buying even the cheapest things with a wheelbarrow full of notes. And lots of zeros being added to each denomination of currency. Here in Zimbabwe it created pauper trillionaires.

I couldn't resist keeping a few notes as souvenirs. I mean, it's not every day you get to hold a 100-trillion dollar note, now is it?

With some help from the World Bank they've now ditched the Zimbabwean dollar in favour of the US dollar and this seems to have stabilized things. You still have people in the streets more keen to take the T-shirt off your back in exchange for the curio you want to buy than to accept a note though. Having been given a 2 US dollar note (huh!) I'm not surprised. Now I know there is a US two-dollar bill but they're as rare as rocking-horse shit so what are they doing in Zimbabwe? I've got a feeling it wasn't printed by the US government!

Anyway, we're in Victoria Falls and this is the end of our overland trip. A farewell dinner later and we're the only two from the trip left in town as everyone has headed back to their home country and working lives.

Relaxing by the pool with a Pimm's and ginger ale (no one seems to have lemonade here, and unfortunately no cucumber either) it's wonderful to reminisce on Southern Africa. A trip that's made new friends, afforded us some memories that will never leave and some sights that will be hard to beat.

Probably the most spectacular of these we only saw yesterday. Stanley was famous for saying 'Dr Livingstone I presume?' What isn't recorded is if he followed it up with 'Bloody hell!' upon gazing at the cataracts that would soon be named Victoria Falls.

Zimbabwe may not currently have a lot of currency on the world stage but one thing won't change and that is people will come to see this no matter what the economic or political chaos. In typical African style there is nothing to stop you from getting as close to the experience as possible and just as the animals see off a few tourists every year, the falls do too. One guy fell off only two months ago.

You can stand on the very edge and gaze into the abyss below. Water hurled over the falls crashes into the rock floor with such force that a fine mist is catapulted back into the air and washes over you intermittently. On a bright sunny day, like the one we were pleased to be enjoying, the most beautiful rainbows are permanently present.

I'm running out of superlatives to describe the things we're seeing on our expeditions around the world and as we're heading off to Iguazu Falls on the border between Brazil and Argentina soon I'll refrain from going over the top (no pun intended) with the Victoria Falls but it does help sum up our African adventure.

Beautiful and brutal all at once.

South America

Peru

Location, location, location

I've always had an interest in real estate ever since my mother told me to buy a house as early in life as possible as it'll always be a good investment over time. I did so, at the age of 21, even though it was crippling in the first few years. Looking back now it was the best piece of investment advice I've ever had.

I learnt over the years as well that a good property was not necessarily the one that looked nice and had a new kitchen. It was the one that was in the right location.

If you go to Lima, that's in Miraflores which is a nice area with a section fronting the ocean atop a rocky cliff, you can sit of an evening at one of a number of lovely little cafés and watch the sunset whilst enjoying a nice vino blanco, *gambas a la plancha* and your better half's company. Everywhere else is either falling down or choking in smog.

If you then travel inland to Cuzco at a breathless 3600 metres ASL you'll want something around the old square. Sure, you'll have to dodge the very lovely young ladies in colourful costumes hawking themselves and a llama for photos and also the not so lovely (and worryingly also very young) ladies selling 'a very good massage' but you'll be in a wonderful old colonial city with great restaurants and bars (the best we frequented in Peru actually) and lots of interesting markets and people. This ancient capital of the Incas also has a number of sacred sites to visit and from these you have a wonderful view of the snow-capped Andes mountains in the distance and the city sitting in a natural bowl below. Strangely, as anything with a view is usually expensive, this high ground is occupied by the poor. They might be living in shacks but they've got one helluva vista to make up for it. Probably why they're smiling and waving as we drive through.

If you find yourself in the south east you'll be at the highest navigable lake in the world – Lake Titicaca. There's a town up here called Puno and to be honest you probably wouldn't need a lot of moolah to buy one of the nicer looking places with a lake view. The most interesting aren't on land though, they're in the middle of the lake. What I mean is they're floating. The Uros people have made a home out of the lake's reeds which is pretty ingenious.

The guide has been trying to convince us that it's because they like it out there but I'm pretty sure it's because the landlubbers historically used to bully them so they moved out of harm's way. They've built everything from houses (well, huts) to a trout farm to their boats to the ground they walk on from reeds. They even eat the stuff. I tried it and it's very refreshing. A little like a cool stick of celery on a summer's day. Put that together with their very colourful clothing and a penchant for eating guinea pig and you've got a pretty memorable place to visit.

The guinea pig is a local delicacy and rather nice by the way. Deep fried, legs akimbo and washed down with the local fire water. There's not a lot of meat but at least you know what it is. Rather than some of the mystery meat we'd been served up in a couple of places on our travels.

Head back north of Cuzco and you'll end up at Aguas Calientes. We took the very stately Hiram Bingham train to reach this high Andes location. It's owned by the Eastern & Orient Express these days and is rather resplendent in royal blue with gold highlights and lettering. It's got an open carriage viewing car at the rear plus a bar, a lounge and a dining room Agatha Christie would have approved of.

The journey is up there with the best you can experience in a train, anywhere in the world. It trundles through the most fetching pampas, river valleys and mountain scenery which gets more and more dramatic the further you go.

You can also take the Inca Trail as an alternative method of reaching our goal but that would have involved tents, a hole and a shovel and as I pointed out in the Introduction to this book that's a non-starter for the missus. Plus, if you ever give your wife the choice of a four-hour train journey with soft seats and champagne or a four-day hike up a mountain I'd like to bet she'll take the former before you even finish uttering the latter. Particularly if you only got married recently.

Now, this town is really nothing to look at, being largely souvenir shops and half-finished motels, but if you look up you'll see what is. You're surrounded on all sides by kilometre-high mountains whose sheer green slopes disappear into cloud forest. Think multiple sugarloaf mountains tightly bunched with a river snaking through the very narrow valley between and you'll get the idea.

You'll need to take one of the frequent (and rather rapidly driven) buses up the somewhat heart-stopping switchback road to the top to find the real gem in Peru's property market. The train we were on was named after the American historian who 'discovered' the 'lost city of the Incas' in 1911. In reality it was never lost to the locals and in my view is the most amazing of all the ancient wonders the world has to offer. It is of course Machu Picchu.

We arrived on a sunny afternoon and checked into the only lodge that's up here. It ain't cheap but believe me when I say it's worth it. The view out of your bedroom window alone could justify the cost. The lowest entrance to the site is also only twenty metres from the lobby and being here to see this place just after sunrise (before the day trippers have arrived) and before sunset (after they've gone again) is truly a special experience.

I've seen Machu Picchu on the TV many a time but actually being here is a little like listening to a CD and then finding AC/DC have just entered your living room to pick up where the last track left off. There is no comparison.

Words and photos do it no real justice. It is awe inspiring and quite simply breathtaking. More so than seeing anything else man's history has assembled, in my view. Sell the wife, pawn the dog and get over here. It's too good for you to miss, no matter what excuses you come up with.

Built in the 1400s it somewhat fell apart after it was abandoned but by the time we visited it'd been spruced up and is just the most arresting sight. There are stone agricultural terraces that step down the mountainside to the point where the slope becomes sheer. There are stone temples, observatories and monuments erected in the names of many a god and the ruling emperor. There are stone living quarters and a working ancient water distribution system. And yes, that's made out of stone as well.

I mention the building material because it's been cut and fashioned into shapes that slide or fit together without the use of mortar or another bonding agent. Frequently on a perilously steep mountain slope. On Wayna Picchu, which is the mountain in the immediate background of any photo you've seen of this place, these buildings seem to defy gravity. It's sides are so steep they carry a hazard warning to anyone climbing them, yet hundreds of metres up above the main citadel of Machu Picchu there are the same houses, temples and terraces. Stone masonry was obviously an important craft and the result is more than impressive.

Now, all of this would be remarkable but what really adds the pizzazz is the location. The backdrop of massive domed peaks is something else and when you've got llamas mowing the grass in the foreground it only makes it even more so. One morning I was up early to see the sunrise breach the mountains and illuminate the city. It wasn't initially what I was hoping for though as all I actually saw was a white-out as cloud drifted all around me. Sitting down at a vantage point I'd been to the day before I was patient and was duly rewarded thirty minutes later with a misty striptease that would be impossible to beat, short of Scarlett Johansson's birthday treat to the lucky bugger who married her.

Small glimpses of green grass and grey stone at first, followed by rays of sunlight piercing the white sky of drifting mist that's so low it's rolling over the ground.

Followed by snapshots of the complete and wondrous scene of what can be achieved when man and nature really try to work as a team.

Sadly, then followed by the day trippers walking through the shot as the cloud evaporates completely but hey, when something this special is in a location like this you'll not be alone for long.

It's what the realty people call a property of immense character with a stunning view. They're not normally known for understating something but in this case they'd be underselling it.

Photography is no substitute for seeing it with your own eyes. Particularly if the photo is reprinted in black and white because you're too cheap to pay for a colour one.

Ecuador

We find ourselves face to face with the great phenomenon — that mystery of mysteries — which is the 1st appearance of new beings on earth (Charles Darwin)

I was reading one of those house and home style magazines before we flew into Quito. Not because I'm particularly interested (although they do have some rather good tips on how to avoid your house interior looking like something the Teletubbies would design) but because it was the only thing in English I'd found in the airport lounge before take-off.

They'd got rather a lot of Christmas decoration suggestions which generally included flashing lights, tinsel, fairies, Santas and rather too much shiny stuff. Arriving at our lodgings I realized the proprietor had been reading the very same article but unlike me had decided it was a good idea.

Thing is, if this Christmas makeover had been done in any other house in Ecuador it would have probably looked like Martha Stewart had gone on a drunken decorating binge with her Hispanic maid but this place was amazing and, just like there's the odd guy who can carry off the leather trouser look, the bloke in charge of this place had scored a home run. I'm not just talking about the decorations now, I mean the whole house. You walk in off a steep cobbled street, leading down into the old town, and straight into a small two-storey courtyard that has had the open space covered with a modern glass roof. Eyes still pointing up, there's a covered walkway going all the way around the rectangular space both upstairs and down. Doors lead off from both floors into various rooms and the room that's to be our bedroom. They've left the old terracotta roof tiles to extend under the glass roof and the effect is lovely. With old cast iron garden furniture and a small fountain as a centrepiece to the courtyard plus plenty of plants and the aforementioned Christmas decorations adorning the walls and walkways you'd think there was a magazine shoot about to be shot. The attention to detail and beautiful furniture throughout the house just made this place the most wonderful we'd stayed in. To make it even better we've got the whole place to ourselves for the two nights we're staying. This exclusivity also meant that we got to spend some time with the two men who own it. And with their absolutely tiny dogs. What a great couple and what an unexpected couple of days. They showed us around the old town and capped the day off by letting us use the roof terrace which has a million-dollar view over Quito and the surrounding mountains.

We're starting to think we should be staying longer as Quito is turning out to be a great find. It has a very well preserved old town from Spanish colonial days and that extends to the opera house which has rather a natty martini bar. But we're here as a stepping stone to the one place on the planet I've wanted to go to since David Attenborough presented it on the BBC more than twenty-five years ago. The Galapagos Islands.

Now, throughout this book I've been trying to put over a tongue-in-cheek approach to conveying the things we've done and seen but I'm probably going to fail in this section and end up waxing lyrical about the place. You see, if you're a nature lover like me you're simply going to have your senses overrun in the enchanted isles. That's the name one Captain Rivadeneira bestowed on the place in the sixteenth century by the way.

There you go, I've started already so you'll just have to humour me for a page or two.

They're volcanic like Hawaii but unlike Hawaii are home to quite the most diverse and in some cases bizarre creatures you're ever likely to meet.

Have you ever thought a penguin would live at the equator? They do here. Having followed the Humbolt current up the Chilean coast from Tierra del Fuego and the Southern Ocean they couldn't swim back against it and got stuck on the islands. The same goes for virtually all the larger mammals and reptiles which would have either swum or floated over on vegetation rafts. Even the birds, which would have arrived here on the trade winds, in a lot of cases couldn't fly back.

These species had to adapt to life on the islands, and some of them are now the famous face of the place that inspired Charles Darwin to theorize about evolution.

The sea lions are one of the first creatures we see. We had to step over two to get onto the dinghy that was taking us out to our yacht. And this was going to be a very frequent experience – trying not to step on the locals – as all the creatures act the same. It's got something to do with there being so few humans here, and historically none. The animals just don't seem to have any concept that we're dangerous so don't bother moving when you get close. Mind you the giant tortoises couldn't move that fast anyway. At up to half a tonne and with no natural predators I suppose they don't need to. They also live for a rather long time unless a volcanic explosion or a sailor from yesteryear decides to boil them up. Some of them are really old. Think 200 years. We found this out from our guides along with enough additional facts for me to write a book. I can see you're starting to worry! I am trying my best not to end up with an appendix to the *Encyclopedia Britannica* you know.

But I love one of them so much I am going to repeat it.

We met one tortoise that was 180 years old. We'd learned that you can age these grand old half shells a little like trees, by counting the rings on the plates of its shell. More rings, as with trees, means more years. Unfortunately, after fifty years the rings start to meld into each other and it's then not possible to age them accurately. But the scientists were able to predict an accurate age for our new friend by carbon dating the musket ball lodged in the arse end of his suit of armour! The poor bugger had been used for target practice by a soldier some time in the nineteenth century!!. That's one hell of a long time to be carrying shrapnel around.

It was obviously so easy to abuse these animals for fun or kill them for food historically because they either have no defence or simply see no danger in humans. Thankfully, all who visit these days do so only with the intention of shooting photos.

I love boobies

You'd think that the birds would fly off when you get close but they don't. After sailing overnight to our first stop at Genovesa Island we were greeted immediately upon stepping ashore by frigate birds, Galapagos doves and Nazca boobies. They've made nests on the dirt paths used by our guides and are generally waddling around or sitting in the small dead looking (but apparently they're not) bushes and trees that cover the island. You can walk up to them and put your camera within inches of their faces and take the most incredible shots. It's really a unique and in some ways quite surreal experience as you just don't get this anywhere else on the planet. You can't even get this close to animals in a zoo.

Quite a few on our boat have brought massive zoom lenses and rather large binoculars to make sure they get some great close-ups. After a day wildlife spotting though I realize that all you need is a basic digital SLR and no specialist lenses or equipment as the animals *pose* for you. Really. You can actually get them to turn into the camera or walk in a certain direction or just stay still. I've got many a photo of my better half standing or squatting next to a bird or mammal as though they had just come over for a drink and a chat.

I even had frigate birds flying alongside me on several occasions whilst out on a dinghy. The males have the most glorious red bladders attached to their throats that blow up like a balloon. Team this with their batman-like wing silhouette and you've got one great photo subject.

But my favourites were the boobies. And these were a wonderfully regular encounter. They're just so engaging and charming with their slightly cross-eyed look and a trademark elongated and breathless whistle. They make you smile and you can't help but love 'em. There are three types. The fairly plain Nazca which we'd already tripped over on many an occasion, the red-footed which lives in the trees on account of it having developed toes that can grip branches, and the blue-footed which is just the most humorous bird you're ever likely to see. When they do their little dance you'll howl with delight. Beak stretched to the heavens whilst whistling, wings tucked into their sides and bright blue feet alternately raised as far up as they can manage. I'm pretty sure Monty Python stole this for the Ministry of Silly Walks.

This delightful creature was another that historically paid for its friendliness. It's the origin of the phrase 'booby trap' as all you needed was a string fashioned into a noose. You then just walk up to the bird, put the noose on the floor next to it and wait for it to put its foot in. Pull and lunch is served.

They may be a little dumb but once you've seen them I defy you not to fall in love.

The John Travolta of the bird world.

> *There is nothing – absolutely nothing – half so much worth doing as simply messing about in boats.* (Kenneth Grahame, The Wind in the Willows)

The marine life is many and varied out here, too. And we've settled on a journey that will take us across the equator three times and between eight of the archipelago's islands in search of it.

Sailing around from one island to another is such a wonderful experience on its own as I love being out at sea. It's even better when the yacht you're on is an old three-mast fishing boat that's been refitted into a dive boat and gin palace all in one.

The islands are in some cases hundreds of miles apart but generally the lengthy sailing is done overnight so you wake up to a new and exciting island view every day or so. And wake up early at that. 5am most mornings. After a few days I'm starting to think I'm in the Ecuadorian navy. But it's worth it as the majority of the marine life is up and around at sunrise so if you want to see them you'd better be too.

Before you even get into the water you can see plenty. Frequently, with coffee in hand, I'd be looking over the side of the yacht after breakfast and see oceanic sun fish and brighties whales. Once there was even a massive manta ray. I've seen these before whilst diving but never one that was five metres across. Truly awesome. I'd planned ahead for the snorkelling and brought a small underwater camera. And what a decision that turned out to be.

Snorkelling is a daily activity for us and our small group of companions. Not all are as proficient as others so there's a training day where we get to mess around at a most beautiful white sand beach with a very inviting turquoise ocean lapping at its edges. There are angel fish, parrot fish, surgeon fish, gringo fish (named on account of them turning red in the sun) and all manner of others that I haven't learnt the names of yet. But best of all there are sea lions sunning themselves both on the beach and a rocky outcrop nearby.

We've been told to be careful around the bulls as they can be a little feisty but the females and pups are no danger at all. Swimming up to a rocky outcrop with several sea lions basking in the morning sun I can't help myself and start playfully clapping my hands together and making a noise like a sea lion. The most wonderful thing then happens. One of the pups looks at me and slides into the water.

Ducking my head under the surface I see he's right there next to my leg swimming in circles. I dive down a couple of metres to see if he'll stay around and play and he comes right up to my face and blows bubbles at me through his nose! Oh my God, this is magical.

I twist and roll and blow bubbles back through my mask and he does it again. This goes on for some thirty minutes and allows me to get a few incredible photos of quite the most arresting animal I've ever met in the ocean. This turns out to be a daily occurrence as we sail around the archipelago. Eat your heart out Dr Dolittle!

The missus is generally wary of anything larger than a goldfish when she's in the ocean so is a little jumpy the first time I get her into the water to experience this close encounter. And I'm not kidding. There were penguins flying around feeding on small fish and she thought they were out to get her. And don't even get me started on the giant green sea turtles. Probably the most gentle creature in the ocean but most of them were bigger than her so she figured it best to clamber onto my back so there was something between her and them should they decide to 'stampede'.

Thing is, this time she was right about there being things out to get her. After diving down for as long as my breath would hold and then re-surfacing she's crying in pain along with several other snorkellers. They've been stung by jellyfish.

Everyone swims back to the dinghy about twenty metres away and scrambles on board. Seems that we've been unlucky enough to swim into a small number of translucent jellies that float on the surface. They're tiny (hence the reason no one spotted them) and have a sharp sting but nothing worse than that from a nettle. I offer to pee on the swelling (as it apparently gets rid of the sting and the swelling, although I don't actually know anyone who's experienced it) to try and lighten the mood but no one's laughing. I guess that's fair enough as most are stung on the face.

Back on the yacht I figure it's best to find a quiet corner and edit some photos while the walking wounded drain the kitchen of vinegar and the medical cabinet of everything else. A few beers on the sun deck watching the frigate birds harass a couple of red-billed tropic birds until they regurgitate their catch of the day lightens the mood and soon the jelly encounter is assigned to memory ready for the next dinner party.

Descended from the apes! My dear, let us hope that it is not true, but if it is, let us pray that it will not become generally known.' (Wife of the Bishop of Worcester, after she heard about *The Origin of Species*)

Actually it's the 200th anniversary year of Charles Darwin visiting the Galapagos Islands. He wasn't the first but is by far the most famous.

Spending time in this place you can see first-hand how he came to the theory that all creatures have evolved. I read a sizeable chunk of his famous tome during the voyage and found out that it was the island's finches that played a large part in his thoughts. Each had grown a very specific beak shape to specialize in eating a particular berry, seed or other based on the food available on their particular island. The giant tortoises had done the same by developing different shell shapes to suit their particular island habitat and this local variation also extended to maybe the most bizarre creature on these islands. The marine iguana.

Getting up at 5am, again, we headed out on the Zodiac to Fernandina Island. This is the youngest island in the archipelago at a mere half million years and is still very actively volcanic. All of the land is lava rock which makes for fantastic pictures of the rather unusual sally light-foot crabs. Their orange backs and sky-blue bellies clash wonderfully with the obsidian (black rock). Even more striking are the clusters of marine iguanas on the rocky shore all pointing into the rising sun to catch a few rays to warm up the blood. They're a little like me the morning after a night out with the boys at the moment. Rather sleepy and slow to move. It doesn't take them long to get enough heat to get the joints moving though and it seems the first order of the day is to blow snot at each other. Yep, their first act is to squirt salt water through their nostrils at any other male that might be sitting too close or moving in on their gal.

Mostly that's all they do but we did see a couple that hadn't resolved their differences with snot so proceeded to have a head banging competition followed by a few bites from their rather comical fat-lipped mouths. Seeing this really reminded me of one of those 1970s' monster movies where two reptiles have been superimposed onto a backdrop of jungle or desert and appear to be thirty foot tall when in fact they're probably the size of your forearm. And boy did these guys look the part. There would be no need to add additional horns or spikes or other nobbly bits as they're butt ugly. With stub noses to allow them to graze sea grass and long clawed toes so they can hang on to the rocks underwater while doing so these guys are truly the epitome of how to evolve to your surroundings.

Not quite sure why the ones on Espanola Island are bright red and green though. Surely they can't know it's nearly Christmas?!

The Galapagos Islands have so many amazing memories for me. It's certainly not the cheapest place to visit as quite sensibly they use price to keep the numbers down to help preserve this geological and biological wonder. And it's not the easiest to get to being some 1000 kilometres off the west coast of South America but it is one of those places you must go and see.

Charles Darwin came here and ended up changing the field of biology in as great a way as Einstein changed the field of physics. You may not achieve anything comparable but your soul will be enriched in a way only somewhere as special as the enchanted isles can manage.

Argentina

Don't mention the war

Growing up in the UK in the 1970s and 80s, Argentina only registered in my consciousness as the place corned beef came from and that country we were fighting to retain sovereignty of the Falkland Islands.

To this I would then add the now infamous 'hand of God' from Diego Maradona, that knocked England out of the 1986 soccer world cup and saw Argentina go on to win it.

Corned beef doesn't really elicit a response of any emotion out of your average Englishman but mention either of the other two and for anyone who's old enough to remember you will most probably get an opinion. Going to a country where the locals are of a Latin temperament, staunchly patriotic and mad about football will probably mean there's an opinion or two to be had from an Argentine perspective too.

Now, I'm not expecting the locals to be throwing things at me but I am expecting a certain reserve towards my nationality. Hopefully not commencing with a cavity search at the airport.

I needn't have worried though. From the moment we

arrived we couldn't have wished for the locals to be nicer. I'm not saying I've instantly made new lifelong friends or found anyone who thinks the Falklands should remain British (check out any local country map and I guarantee those islands are marked as Las Malvinas, Argentina) but everyone is smiling and even my quite terrible Spanish is patiently listened to and I normally get the thing I was after without resorting to pointing.

I took a little Spanish when I was eighteen. She was a lovely girl. Taught me how to role my 'r's beautifully, but that was a long time ago and even though I've been to Spain a few times since I've never got much further than basic conversation and ordering a beer. The fact that they speak English down here more than you'd think is therefore a help. But have a go in Spanish, it's fun and appreciated.

You can't help making a European link with the character of the people, and the country, which makes everything sort of familiar too. You even get this in the tropical north east of the country where we first landed.

Iguazu is the home of the legendary waterfalls. We're spending Christmas here and having now had a few days to take in the splendour of this natural marvel I'd be hard pressed to immediately think of a more spectacular and relaxed setting to enjoy my turkey and stuffing.

We've just recently visited Southern Africa's famous falls and I have to say that Iguazu is head and shoulders better as a spectacle. That's not to say you shouldn't go and see Victoria Falls as it's rather impressive, as detailed in a previous chapter, it's just that Iguazu gives you the impression it's been created by someone who thinks legalizing marijuana is a good idea.

Why have one waterfall when you can have twenty? Why have the water dropping 100 metres to the river below when you can have it cascading? Why have only water and rock when you can have jungle, right up to and over the edge, and birds and butterflies of every colour. And, and, and ...

It's a movie backdrop Indiana Jones would be proud of. With no need for special effects.

You can go see it from the bottom, in a boat (which as part of the price will take you close enough to the torrent of falling water that you'll get a shower), and halfway up on trails where the butterflies are as big as your hand and the trees are filled with giant cicadas strumming a background chorus. And finally, you can view it all from the top, on a man-made catwalk that takes you right to the edge. Don't leave without doing all three as each gives a unique perspective and the overall memory will be that much more complete.

And the best bit is that after you've spent the day wandering around taking photos and generally shaking your head in wonder you can retire to your hotel room balcony with a very nice glass of Malbec and watch it from the comfort of your chair, as the sun sets over the water, mist drifting slowly up into the air.

Patagonia

Perhaps one day, tired of circling the world, I'll return to Argentina and settle in the Andean lakes ... (Ernesto 'Che' Guevara, *The Motorcycle Diaries*)

Iguazu Falls was a wonderful highlight on our trip but we really came to Argentina to visit Patagonia.

The southern cone of South America with an Andean backbone is one of the world's last great wildernesses and it having the claim to being the end of the world, before you hit Antarctica, just adds to the mystique.

Having spent New Year enjoying the wines and tree-lined streets of old Mendoza and a quick visit to Aconcagua to see South America's tallest mountain, the trek south that will end in Ushuaia, Tierra del Fuego soon sees us passing through the provinces of Neuquen, Rio Negro and Chubut on our way to Santa Cruz.

All have their sights and diversions. Hugging the western Andes it's not difficult to find a spectacular snow-covered mountain or a lake of pure turquoise that glistens in the sun.

One of our favourites was Villa Pehuénia at the northern end of Lanin National Park, mainly because very few have yet to find it and the *cabañas* and *hosterias* there have a homely individual feel that can only be had pre-commercialization. The area also has a lot of monkey puzzle trees, known as Pehuéns locally (hence the name of the area). Go find it before everyone else does!

Bariloche and the lake district are not to be missed either but commercialization has definitely arrived in this most favourite of Argentine holiday resorts. You'll enjoy the mountains, lakes and local chocolate aplenty, but will have to share (not the chocolate) with a large number of people.

Our next favourite stop south was Alerces National Park outside of Esquel in Chubut. Esquel is the home of the Patagonian Express – the last of the original steam trains that used to criss-cross the region in times gone by. As luck would have it we stayed at a bed and breakfast lodge of the guy who's written a famous book on it. And his wife made the most wonderful cakes. This town is small and not touristy and still has livestock markets every week. And it's all the better for it.

Outside of town there's also no real commercialization, just mile after mile of stunning forest, mountain and lake scenery. We went across Lago Menendez to see the 2500-year-old Alerces trees and, would you believe, a bamboo forest. Yes, bamboo in the Andes. I thought this stuff only grew naturally in China. Here's a thought though. If China is having trouble finding habitat for its pandas then maybe they could send a few over here. Virtually no people and quite the most pristine environment, and there were so many places you could drive or hike to where you could comment similarly.

We haven't seen mountain scenery like this since we left New Zealand. In fact, we're now at a similar latitude so maybe it's not surprising.

Donde esta la gasolina?!

The further south you go, generally, the windier it gets and more desolate. And when the wind blows down here it really blows. We were lucky enough to get a majority of light wind, sunny days but on the few it rained (horizontally) and the wind was making the ubiquitous corrugated metal roofs rattle it was best to stay inside and enjoy a *maté*. It's a local drink that everyone's addicted to. You see people drinking it everywhere all of the time. And there isn't even any alcohol or caffeine in it. Essentially a tea, it appears to be a cultural and social backbone to life down here.

The term *maté*, I found out from a local who showed us how to prepare it, refers to both the herb used and the small cup it's taken in. Essentially you make it by taking a good handful of chopped and dried herb, adding hot water (not boiling by the way, this is a sacrilege and will have the locals wailing at you as though you've just wiped your nose on their shirt) and after a short while sucking it up through a metal straw which has a sieve at the bottom to stop the leaves from being sucked up too. Oh, and the cup is normally made from a small pumpkin gourd. Delightfully weird, and just the sort of thing that feels right at home in a part of the world where gauchos roam the hillsides on sheepskin-saddled horses. Herding goats.

Leaving the Chubut valley where the Welsh set up home, back in the eighteenth century, and Butch Cassidy and the Sundance Kid holed up for a few years (yep, they were real people), you quickly feel the human head count decreasing. There are a lot of one-man towns around here. I'd normally use the term 'one-horse town' but there are seemingly more of those than people. They're everywhere. You also see quite a lot of choique (think half sized emu with a turn of speed that would embarrass a greyhound) and guanaco (think fluffy llama).

Which is more than can be said for petrol stations. There's one about every 200 kilometres, from what we experienced. This is good enough to allow a fill up before you have to start pushing the car but still far enough apart for you to need to do some forward planning. The problem though is that when you get to the station, and assuming you can find it as they're not lit up with neon-lights or even at the roadside most of the time, they frequently haven't got any fuel. So you can easily be on the road for more than 400 kilometres getting sweaty palms because of the imminent possibility of running out. Under such circumstances the decision to turn off the air-conditioning to save fuel is an easy one. Even if the missus needs persuading that getting sweaty is better than getting stranded.

On three separate occasions I was greeted by a petrol pump attendant (yes, they still do this for you down here, which is great) shaking his head and telling me he had no fuel today. This is when you start to get nervous even though you had the foresight to buy a petrol can and fill it, back at the start of the trip, as an emergency back-up for the time you might get caught short. But what to do when that's also run out?

Well, there are people out here even though they are few and far between. And they have cars which obviously run on fuel, was the logic I found myself using. So a spot of light begging a couple of times got us out of a hole. Nice people these Patagonians.

Mind you, if I was out here again, I'd have at least two fuel cans and at least two spare tyres as a minimum. Plus at least five litres of water. At all times.This may sound like overkill but my experience now tells me it should be a basic if you want to avoid a very miserable delay to your holiday.

A journey into the middle of nowhere needs a spot of detailed planning and a bit of luck. Both saved us on a couple of occasions.

Ruta 40

Let's face it though, these days it's easier to do this trip than it must have been back in the time of Che Guevara.

Ernesto 'Che' Guevara is that bloke with the beret on a million T-shirts across the planet. You know the one I mean. It's normally a printed silhouette with a communist star background and is the poster child of rebellious teens throughout the world. If you ever go to Havana in Cuba you'll see the same image on the wall overlooking the main parade square. Him and Fidel Castro were big mates.

He's dead now but back in the day, when he wasn't helping Fidel embarrass the Americans or stoking revolution elsewhere in South America, he did a spot of travelling. He famously rode a motorbike from the north of South America to the south with a large chunk of the trip passing through Argentina. He had a splendid time, as we are now doing, and kept a diary that's available as a book and has recently been made into a film.

The Argentines hadn't got around to the idea of tarmac at the time so he had somewhat of an adventure on ripio. Ripio is the name given to the roughly hewn tracks that pass as roads that are prevalent along the Andes side of Argentina. If you're lucky they have a compressed earth and gravel surface. If you're not, they're a collection of ruts and potholes you could hide a small horse in.

And that's without even mentioning the rocks strewn everywhere. These range from fist-sized ones that thud off the underside of your vehicle to football-sized ones that you bounce off if you're unlucky enough to hit one.

The road Che Guevara took is the famous Ruta 40 and it's the same one we're using to travel south. It's still largely ripio. Now, you may be thinking, well, it's just a car journey. And if some bloke with a beret can do it in the 1950s on a motorbike then it can't be that hard. And in some ways you'd be right. We passed several guys attempting at least a section of it on pushbikes. And several in 1960s' and 70s' cars. You can even take a bus (although this takes a longer route around some of the more challenging sections).

If it was going to be as tough as, say the Dakar Rally, then I probably wouldn't have hired a faux 4x4 for the task. And I'd have also hired a few back-up options. Say, a satellite phone and a repair crew.

But this trip isn't to be taken lightly as there is no mobile phone coverage for hundreds of kilometres at a time and also no sign of civilization for very long periods. And to get from one place to another takes a minimum of six hours and sometimes as much as twelve. By the time we gave the hire car back at the end of the trip we'd covered 8000 kilometres.

You could get into trouble out here.

And we did.

You start to get confident in your ability to four-wheel slide on the loose surface, which is great fun, and after a while your speed starts to creep up. The road disappears to a heat haze horizon for mile after mile and you get into a trance driving, if you're not careful. Unlike normal roads not all curves are marked and there's often no warning about upcoming hazards.

Like the deserted roadworks around the next bend.

What I mean actually is road surface scraping, to try and fill in the potholes, and moving some of the dangerous rocks out of the way of unsuspecting motorists coming round the corner. Having been abandoned that hadn't yet happened.

I was quick enough to miss the really big boulders but smacked one that was big enough to break something. The sound was sickening as granite met metal. Coming to a halt I was sure we were in trouble. The last town was some sixty kilometres ago and the next one was over a hundred into the distance.

Earlier we'd passed a guy in a truck whose rear axle had fallen off. The road surface had fatigued the chassis to breaking point and it had just fallen apart. He told us he was okay and a tow truck would come and get him tomorrow. We offered him some water and food but he seemed to be prepared. Almost as though he'd been in this position before.

Were we about to be sleeping in our car for a night too?

Well, my luck must have been in the stars because we'd managed to escape disaster, saved by the long travel suspension of the car which had soaked up the worst of the impact. I made a mental note to myself there and then that I would now always hire an SUV style car when travelling on poor roads. We had a dent the size of an egg in the front nearside wheel but the tyre hadn't punctured and didn't seem to be deflating. As we only had one spare and the dented wheel and tyre appeared to be holding I decided to keep going on it. My logic was if I put the spare one on and got a puncture then I'd be relying on a tyre that by that time may have deflated. Best to keep running on the damaged one at low speed until it could be fixed and if it did deflate then go for the spare. So, heart now descended from mouth back into its correct place we gingerly continued until the next town.

We made it and in my broken Spanish, and with the

help of a lot of pointing and sound effects, the rather large and swarthy mechanic got the message and fixed my dented wheel. With a lump hammer.

After he'd finished bashing the wheel a few seconds of silence passed between us as he looked up at me, half-smoked cigarette hanging from his lips and plumber's bottom winking at me from his jeans, and I looked back at him. I asked if it was okay to drive on and he replied with a nonchalant shrug and a smile '*Si*'.

So we hopped back in and kept going. A little more cautiously this time.

Well, at least for the first hour.

Best to know what you're doing out here as you'll be waiting a very long time for the Automobile Association to come and help!

Glaciers and Amigos

And there was more to come.

On a positive note first though, would you believe we managed to meet up with a friend out here in the wilds? He was taking the bus south (partly along Ruta 40) to El Chalten and El Calafate in the Santa Cruz region where we were headed. It was great to meet up in such a foreign place and he'd brought along a Peruvian girlfriend which made speaking Spanish to third parties much easier for the rest of the journey.

After a night of meat and Malbec we'd talked them into swapping their glacially slow bus for the back seat of our car and the next day the four of us were off.

And it took us all of fifty kilometres to get a puncture. Well, more of a tyre wall blowout actually. And of course it happened on a dusty windswept hill in the middle of nowhere.

With a spare pair of hands we had it changed in twenty minutes though and were off again. But this is where you realize how easy it is to get into danger. We now had no spare tyre and were on a 700-kilometre trip down a dirt track the participants of the Dakar Rally would be cautious on. In fact, it's highly possible they are travelling on some similar stretch of road as the Dakar is running in Argentina and Chile this year. During this week. Something to do with potential terror attacks making it too dangerous to run in West Africa.

But I digress. There were only two towns between us and El Chalten. Neither had a tyre that would fit our car.

As luck would have it we made it without further problems though, and were treated to quite the most arresting sight you're likely to see upon entry into a town.

Fitzroy Mountain towers over the tiny frontier hamlet of El Chalten. At this end of Lago Viedma you meet the edge of a weather pattern. The blue-sky sunny side we were driving the lake's 100-kilometre long coast on, giving way to wind and dark clouds as the mountains start to rise.

The wind was really blowing and you could feel it through the steering of the car. When we stopped to take a few photos the girls were almost blown off their feet. This change of weather was the thing that was about to give us the stunning view I mentioned. As we stood there clicking a few frames Fitzroy appeared imposingly through the clouds, like a cruise liner drifting out of a misty ocean. As they say, timing is everything.

We stayed at an *estancia* for the next few nights. It's the Patagonian version of a farm. Estancia La Quinta was the only inhabited settlement in this area until the 1980s when a border dispute with Chile saw El Chalten founded. It's still a very small settlement and was one of our favourite spots on the whole trip.

The *estancia* was something of a treat. It's a working farm with Hereford cattle and is still run by the family that have owned it for many generations. This made for interesting tales of an evening, such as the one about Long Jack, the first white guy to live in this area who thought he'd made his fortune when he found a rock that appeared to be a fossilized human skull. But turned out to be just a rock. Got laughed out of town, the poor chap.

It was the view of the sky at night devoid of light pollution that made it so special for me though. A veritable ecstasy of stars and constellations was on show in a deep blue-black sky. I even saw a couple of shooting stars. Heaven.

El Chalten. Small town, BIG scenery!

Big Ice

There are only two places that have larger ice fields than Patagonia. One's the Arctic and the other is the Antarctic. It's not surprising then that the glacial activity here is a sight to behold, and the most impressive of these is Perito Moreno from what I've seen.

This glacier is not to be confused with Perito Moreno town, by the way. Perito Moreno glacier is something you'll travel out of your way to see. Perito Moreno town is strangely nowhere near the glacier and just somewhere you have to stop on your way south as the distances, north or south, to the next warm bed and hopefully full tank of fuel are just too big.

So you'll see both if you're travelling Ruta 40 but it'll be the glacier you'll remember. It's stunningly beautiful and quite the most accessible lump of ice you're likely to find anywhere on the planet. The face of it pushes up against a peninsula of land with two halves of the same lake on either side. The amount of ice forming at the top of the glacier in the Andes is roughly equal to the amount falling off the front face at the lake (meaning it's not receding) so it's always easy to see, being only about 200 metres away at the closest point from the extensive viewing areas the park services have thoughtfully erected. It then stretches up to four kilometres left and four kilometres right to push up against the valley walls. 200 metres sounds like a long way but when you consider the glacier is as high as a twenty-storey building it feels like you can almost touch it.

Now, just being this close to a glacier the size and beauty of this beast is great but when you can also watch great chunks of ice falling off into the lake on a daily basis it's even better. I should say many times a day and sometimes even a few times an hour. We came three separate days to see the spectacle, it's that wonderful.

Looking at the face of the glacier you can clearly see fissures, cracks and chasms that glow an icy blue thanks to the laws of light refraction. The force of ice pushing down from the mountains and that of the lake waters undermining the face result in great shards of ice cracking off. It's a special thing to see. An air-splitting roar is followed by many tonnes of glacier falling into Lago Argentino and a plume of white water marking the splashdown.

You can get even closer to the action on a boat and if you're feeling energetic you can go and hike on the glacier. I was. Obviously, they take you onto a piece of

ARGENTINA

the glacier away from the face but it's no less dramatic. The fissures and chasms you can see from afar are even more spectacular when you're standing on the edge of them.

Crampons fitted to the bottom of your boots stop you from sliding in and also let you climb around ice walls, mounds and troughs without looking like Bambi on an ice rink. There are massive waterfalls in some of the chasms and across a lot of the surface there are little streams. The water is pure and leaning down to take a drink is a great experience. It's ice cold (well obviously) and as fresh as the air up here.

And when you've finished enjoying what Jack Frost has made you can stay down the road in El Calafate where they've got plenty of bars and restaurants and a great view of Lago Argentino from the other end. Our place was perched on a hill right on the lakeside and made for a very relaxing spot to return to after a day out.

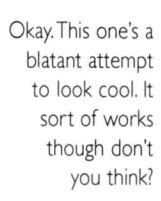

Okay. This one's a blatant attempt to look cool. It sort of works though don't you think?

(and a little bit of)
Chile

Now you see it, now you don't

The Chileans have got some pretty spectacular mountains and glaciers too.

The pick of these has to be those in Torres del Paine national park. It's right in the heart of southern Patagonia on the opposite side of the Andes to Perito Moreno glacier, which made for an interesting trip.

After a lovely week eating well, drinking well and catching up with our friends we said '*hasta luego*' and headed out of El Calafate and across the border to Chile. It's a four-hour bumpy ride through some of the most incredibly strong winds I've experienced anywhere, via the low Andes and a valley pass, into southern Chile but on reaching the other side we were greeted with a wind-free view of mountains and lakes that replaced the Argentine wind for taking your breath away. Perfect sunny conditions confirmed that the postcards you see of this place haven't been photo-shopped because we were now looking at the exact same postcard-quality vistas.

Our little Fiat was struggling with the ripio roads but

managed to get us safely to our hotel in the Serrano river valley. We'd had to swap cars in El Calafate as the faithful Ford we'd travelled the length of Argentina with didn't have a pass to allow it to travel internationally.

What an afternoon we'd picked to arrive. We stopped the car along the road and got out to enjoy the fresh air and incredible view. We were seeing Torres del Paine just as my camera liked it. Imposing, majestic, clearly visible and beautifully lit in the afternoon sun. Massive blue granite horned peaks bordered to the far left and left by the Grey and French Glaciers respectively, all draped with wisps of white cloud in an azure sky. A milky jade coloured lake in the foreground.

We didn't know it at the time (as the map in our guide book was short on detail and we were relying on local signs to get us to the hotel) but we were driving a famous route through the park that skirted the main attractions. We were heading south and seemed to be stopping every kilometre to snap another batch of photos, the route was just so scenic. It took us nearly a further two hours to get to Rio Serrano lodge but not before we'd seen some of the most beautiful mountain scenery Chilean Patagonia has to offer. The final stretch of road afforded us the last photo of the day as we crossed the river and rattled our way up a very badly potholed and corrugated ridge before dropping down into the valley again and our hotel. The ridge had a stunning panoramic view of the park with the sun's rays illuminating the sweeps of the river in the foreground. A great memory to head into a shower and dinner with.

Unfortunately it didn't last and upon waking the next morning and pushing back the curtains we were greeted with somewhat of a different mood. The weather had switched 180 degrees and we now only had mist, rain and a windy chill to experience. Sleet was trying its best to make an appearance too. It was a good job we took some photos yesterday as we never saw the famous view of Torres del Paine again. In five days! I even joked with the hotel staff after day 2 of rain and misted grey-white skies, '*Donde esta Torres del Paine?*' with a shrug. It was as though it had vanished.

Obviously not wanting to stay indoors all day we ventured out but never took one of the more interesting long hikes I'd planned because the hotel staff had told us (and a guest had confirmed it after ignoring their advice) that it would be an exercise in futility as we'd see nothing in this weather. It would also guarantee a thunderstorm on my better half's face too. We did make it to Lago Grey though to see the Grey Glacier. This one was well named by the way. Grey sky, grey water, grey hills and even a grey spit of sand and grey pebbles to cross to see the Grey Glacier. It took a while to poke its head out across the lake and the wind wasn't helping our resolve to wait for it to do so but it did confirm that sometimes you can get a great photo when the weather's less than perfect.

There were several groups who came and went during the time we stayed here and they must have been pissed. This park isn't exactly what you call cheap or easily accessible and to come here and see little or nothing but mist and rain would probably put a dent in your holiday spirit.

It seems we'd been fortunate to see the sights throughout southern Patagonia. Yes, we'd had our fair share of bad weather too but the good days in Torres del Paine, El Calafate and El Chalten had more than made up for those. We'd met people on the road after visiting each and they said they'd only got wind, rain and clouds when they were there. Upon showing them a few photos of what sits behind the weather shroud they'd experienced their eyes would light up and a request for a copy of a few photos would rapidly follow. I was happy to oblige.

The same was true of Perito Moreno glacier. We needed sunscreen more than our raincoats but you needed to take both irrespective of what the weather report or poking your head outside seemed to be telling you. The weather here is up and down more than a whore's drawers on pay day.

You have to come to southern Patagonia regardless because whether the weather gods smile on you or not, Mother Nature's masterpieces down here are worth it. It's one of those places you need to see. It's that special.

Getting up early, patiently waiting and returning to the same place a few times on different days will also help. Or just do the opposite of us and come in the winter. It's bloody cold but apparently it's not windy and there are clear skies nearly every day.

(and back to) Argentina

Fin del Mundo

Tierra del Fuego is about as far south as you can go before you hit Antarctica. Technically it's a group of islands which are split between Chile and Argentina. We wanted to go to the most southerly point you could reach by road so opted to cross back to Argentina and headed for Ushuaia.

Having found the sign that marks 'the end of the world' and taken a photo we drove on to visit Estancia Harberton. This place is about eighty kilometres out of town and is slightly further south than Ushuaia. It's still a working farm but also offers local tea and cakes and a great view across the Beagle Channel. It's been home to the same family since it was founded in the late 1800s. The founder was the same chap who founded the settlement that became Ushuaia, a British missionary named Thomas Bridges.

We hadn't got a boat so weren't going to make it to the Chilean islands (and Cape Horn) that lie south of here but it did appear that we'd found the last place you could drive to. Until we spotted a sign pointing further south east down a dirt track. So we took it.

This road was Ruta 40-style ripio with even bigger potholes and ruts in it if that was possible. It also had the added danger of several rickety old bridges crossing various streams and rivers, the wooden surfaces of which should have been replaced a very long time ago. There were no cars down here that we had seen so I stopped at each to make sure they weren't about to collapse. They all turned out to be stronger than they looked thankfully.

We found a simple lighthouse and a beautiful beach some sixty kilometres along. We weren't sure whether we were now indeed further south than Estancia Harberton but nevertheless we'd reached about as far as you could go without swimming. Our final southerly point in the bag, we started to head back to town.

There were a couple of German hikers thumbing a lift all the way down here. They'd been hiking around Tierra del Fuego for weeks and had decided they'd rather not spend another week walking back to Ushuaia. I was happy to help plus they had some useful tips on which sights to spend time seeing and which ones were okay to miss.

The town itself was one that wasn't to be missed as it's in a pretty impressive setting. You first get a stunning view of this when you fly in as the airport is on the southern coast and before you land the view is quite arresting. Ushuaia is built on a natural harbour and the low hills that lead up into a northerly backdrop of snow-covered mountains. There's even a glacier (Martial) that sits high above the town. When you add in a multitude of very colourful houses in the foreground you've got a picture-postcard location if ever I saw one.

This is the town that Antarctic expeditions embark from. It's also a fishing town. And the local delicacy is king crab. Oh goody. The *hosteria*'s receptionist knew which restaurants had the best and it then didn't take us long to get down there and gorge on quite the sweetest and freshest king crab I can ever remember eating. They had some lovely Patagonian vino blanco to help you further enjoy it, the sun was shining every evening and after weeks away from the ocean it seemed just so right.

It made a very nice change to grilled meat and had me slobbering like Pavlov's dog every evening for three days.

Hot in the city

I love coffee. Specifically, I love espresso. And if I can find somewhere that looks like it knows what it's doing my absolute favourite is a macchiato. That little bit of foamed milk on the top of a strong espresso makes it just so. Mind you, in my experience it's harder than you might think to find a really good one. And I'm talking globally here.

Sure, the Italians have it sussed and in exporting their lovely espresso machines all over the world you'd think everyone else would too. Particularly as you can pick up good quality ground coffee virtually anywhere these days. But it's just not the case. I've lost count of the number of times I've gone into a café or coffee shop and come out feeling disappointed.

The coffee is either too weak, too bitter, burned or in some cases not even what I ordered. A case in point is trying to order my favourite macchiato first in Malaysia and secondly in Australia.

What arrived from my Malaysian barista was most definitely a latte. When I pointed this out he said with a smiling face, 'Oh ... this is a Malaysian macchiato.' Trying not to appear as though I was about to ram it down his throat for such a stupid comment I asked him what a Malaysian latte might look like then. He said it was similar and walked off. So did I, before the bill arrived.

Something similar happened in Adelaide at a specialist coffee shop with a barista all the way from Norway (studying in the local university, I was assuming). It and he looked the part and he nodded knowingly when I ordered an espresso macchiato. He was still nodding when he delivered a latte. Feeling a sense of déjà vu I felt the need to point out he was serving me a latte to which he shrugged and said, 'This is how we make it here.' I made a comment that referenced his need to try harder at school and left.

Now, you might by this time be surmising that the coffee in Argentina is crap. Well, no it isn't. I haven't once received a latte or any other form of coffee other than the espresso I've ordered. In Spanish. Badly. So Argentina then, it seems, has got a gold star for getting one of my favourite things right. Perhaps it's the Italian blood in the locals.

It's a pity that the consistent quality of the coffee doesn't seem to apply to the beef. Heresy I hear you cry!

The Argentines have the best steak in the world. Well, the Japanese may argue with that one but it's true that Argentina has somewhat of a reputation for a damn good steak. I've had plenty in places as far flung as Hong Kong, Amsterdam and New York. And they were really good.

But in the more than a month I've been driving virtually the full length of the country (and boy is it a big country) I can count the good steaks I've had on one hand. Now, the good ones did have my soul singing hallelujah. They melted in my mouth and delivered a taste that made my body say thank you for swallowing that. But the others ranged from being good steak that was cooked badly to poor steak that was poor whether it was cooked correctly or not. How can this be? How could a brand so well managed on the world stage be so inconsistent in its birthplace?

Hiking around various parts of the Andes you get to talk to many a like-minded traveller and generally they are locals. Quite a few, surprisingly to me at first, agreed with my comment about the quality of the steak. The most common view on why this travesty was occurring was that the good stuff was being exported. Pity they're not keeping enough for use at home as visitors to Argentina are expectant!

Just as with my pursuit of good coffee, a good steak is worth the trouble and I've not given up on finding it. Having reached Buenos Aires my expectation is higher than ever. It's the capital and our final stop in Argentina before heading north to Brazil.

Boy is it hot here. We seem to have hit a heatwave. Good job there are a lot of gelato shops and the air-conditioning is working in our room.

They speak Spanish in Argentina, but here the feeling you get is that they've also got an Italian side. And it's not just the gelato and espresso. Slang words are Italian and so are greetings. You hear '*ciao*' a lot. I'm also reliably informed swearing is in Italian. The pasta's good too.

There's a strong feeling of Europe here. Baroque

buildings reminiscent of Paris. Tree-lined avenues and squares you'll find in many parts of Barcelona. And the odd 1920s' café that's not unlike those places that time has passed by in Rome and Venice. Not surprising given the history of the immigrants of course.

These delightful details though are not as prevalent as I'd like. Modernization, decades past, seems to have deprived the city of a solid architectural identity. That said, the city has some real gems (including a cemetery bizarrely) and if you're coming to Argentina it's worth taking a few days to mooch around and try out a few cafés, bars and street markets in town whilst casting an eye over them. The real mojo of the city seems to be nocturnal though, so get some rest in the day. After a few days here you'll be struggling not to need a siesta of an afternoon.

Recoleta and Palermo suburbs have a lovely Soho feel and if you can keep awake long enough you'll bump into a party. But don't expect to see the locals tango dancing in the streets. The youngsters don't seem to be interested in something that their grandparents found hip and the grandparents don't hit the plazas as frequently as they used to. Sure you can go and see a show but that's not really a cultural 'beat' that the guidebooks will have you believe flows through the city. Mind you, the Malbec helps you get in the groove.

So does a welcome re-appearance of bloody good steak. After weeks of all too regular disappointment I'm happy to report that Buenos Aires has stepped up and saved Argentina's reputation. It's that good that I spent a small fortune trying as many cuts as my stomach could manage. And after my taste buds were satisfied I took a day to shop and ordered another part of the cow. A very nice leather jacket to add to my wardrobe.

And the best bit was that the tailor-made jacket didn't cost a lot more than the meal the night before.

A damn good deal

Argentina is a different place to what it was even eight years ago. Until the first few years of this century military dictatorships, a constantly collapsing economy and political corruption (sometimes all three at the same time) hampered a country that should long ago have been much wealthier than it is.

It's not difficult to get an opinion out of the locals on their country and everyone we spoke too had a view on politics that didn't take much prompting to surface. Seems the general feeling is that 'a bunch of pirates' are running the place. I've not spotted any eye patches or parrots and all seems well on the streets but I guess the population expects more than rolling economic failure for the masses. Reasonable enough, and it's probably not surprising then that Argentines are a little sceptical about the future, but it's not really keeping the mood down too much.

Argentina is a truly beautiful part of the world and now more than ever it's the locals who are on the road exploring it. Sure, you'll find Americans, Australians, Europeans and Asians hiking up mountains and hitting the bars and restaurants but it's the Argentines that make up the real numbers. And not just hitch-hiking teenagers (although there are a huge number of those). Families, couples and groups of friends of all ages are exploring. No doubt the weakness of the currency and the excellent affordability of Argentina as a whole help this decision but having spent many weeks here now I have to say it would still be a good choice even if it weren't so cheap.

Although, being so far away, unless you're South American it's not really the sort of place you could go to for a long weekend. So take the plunge, save up your holidays and pesos and come on over for a month. You'll be pleased that you did!

Brazil

Samba town

The first time I saw the Rio Carnival Roger Moore was being chased by a bloke with metal teeth. Colourful costumes and colourful people, dancing to a samba beat, made up the backdrop to Mr Bond succeeding to survive yet again. And that image of beautiful people, beautiful beaches, day-long parties and jiggling girls in indecently small bikinis sort of stuck with me.

Not being one to deny myself certain pleasures in life it was high time I made it to the Carnival to see if it really is as good as they say it is. So here we are for a few days of hedonism and (expected) hangovers in the self-proclaimed carnival capital of the world.

I've got to admit that the plan was to turn up and walk out into the street and join the party. But it seems it's not quite that straightforward. For a start, whilst our hotel is on the beach it's about three kilometres away from the nearest street party. Have you ever tried to get a cab on New Years Eve? Anywhere? Well Carnival ain't any different. Getting the missus to walk that far in her heels would be an exercise in futility too. I guess I should have seen this one coming.

The second problem is that the party isn't in one

place, like it is up the road in Salvador for example. We didn't go there but saw it on TV. Two million people samba dancing down the high street. This was what we were looking for in Rio. It didn't seem to exist though.

Rio is a large city and the street parties were dotted about everywhere. This meant that you never saw more than a few thousand people in one place at one time. I did find a nice street parade in Ipanema that didn't resemble 'Spring break' too much. The local bands had a great musical beat and the beer was flowing freely with the crowd. In addition to this you could go and see the main Carnival parade or buy a ticket for a Carnival ball at one of the big hotels. Very confusing for someone who just wants to experience *the* party!

So, now I've been here for a couple of days and experienced the good and bad of it all here's a quick rundown of what's what. As I've commented above, the Carnival is broken down into three different parties. And you're going to need deep pockets to pay for two out of three of them.

The one you see on the TV is the Sambadrome Carnival parade. Then you have the balls, and finally the street parties. All are a competition in one-upmanship which is great when you're spectacting.

Take the main Carnival parade. It's made up of different samba schools from each of the districts of Rio. Everyone is singing, dancing, drumming and parading around their float. These floats are colossuses. A bit more impressive than the things you're likely to have experienced in any county fair you saw as a kid. All are themed and apparently can cost up to one million dollars each! That's a lot of dosh for a paper maché giant whatever, some feathers, a strobe light and half a tonne of glitter.

But actually, they are impressive and the samba troupe that surrounds each one has the effect of bringing it to life. This is the big competition for bragging rights for the next twelve months. From what I can make out though it's also a competition to see how gay the guys can look, in outfits that Liberace would approve of, and how naked the girls can look, in outfits I approve of! A lot of the costumes give you the feeling that the designers were thinking 'Alice in Wonderland meets Willy Wonka's Oompa-Loompas, with a hint of Elton John à la Marie Antoinette'.

We didn't go to the balls but they're all about eating, drinking, dancing and meeting people. You dress up more conservatively for these apparently. No need for sequined hot pants (and that's just the boys).

And finally, the street parties. Lots of samba band parades, lots of people and lots of booze. And this is the only free one out of the three.

There's a schedule for the start and location of each street parade and this is where it starts to fall apart. You see, the locations are spread out over the whole city and the timings aren't exactly accurate from what we experienced. Could you believe it though, they all STOP well before midnight! That's right, the Rio Carnival street parties stop before midnight! What the f#@*? We're not thirteen and we don't have to wake up for school tomorrow you know!

Seems the residents in the famous neighbourhoods don't like the noise and disruption. So the party is confined to the balls and the Sambadrome after the witching hour. Unbelieveable. So make sure you start early if you want to party in the streets as you'll be finishing early.

Both Copacabana and Ipanema are on the seafront

so you could also start your party at one of their beaches. There's plenty of cold beer and of course the famous Brazilian flesh on show. Pity it's not all as compact as the swimwear though.

There are definitely a few potential Miss World contestants breezing around, which for any red-blooded male is a lovely thing, but there are also a fair few potential Miss Dunkin' Donuts contestants too. Which makes you wonder why they're wearing the same size bikinis as the Miss World crowd. It also reinforces your resolve to lay off the fast food.

What amazed me though was their ability to sit out in the sun all day. Male, female, young and old. Where most Europeans (and Caucasians in general) have come to realize sitting in scorching sunshine is a quick way to wrinkled skin and potentially a good dose of skin cancer, Brazilians seem to see it as an elixir of life. Add in a beach and the ocean and they're all as happy as the proverbial pig in mud.

I have a complexion designed for rainy northern Europe and hence turn a lovely red colour after, oh somewhere in the ballpark of say, ten seconds of tropical sun. I'm therefore the guy who's most likely to be wearing factor 30 sunscreen and a hat. This lot aren't really wearing anything and making little to no effort to stay out of the 40 Celsius midday sun. This Englishman isn't joining the mad dogs this week.

Thing is though, the actual Carnival has turned out to be like one of those things you remember fondly from your youth that when revisited just isn't as good as you remember. For example, I loved the TV show *The A-Team* when I was a kid. Particularly the van with the big wheels and red stripe, and all the shooting and action. I made the mistake of watching it again when I was in my thirties. The magic just wasn't there. You could see all the faults (how come no one ever got shot even though they all had automatic weapons?) and the fact that the whole series only had one plot. I love James Bond, but if you go back and watch the ones from the seventies they're not quite as dynamic, sexy and enthralling as you remember.

We went to Rio expecting a full-on party on our doorstep, full of scantily clad ladies in feather headdresses and bare buttocks a race horse would be proud of jiggling their booty along with guys dressed in white and banging away on samba drums.

In reality, it's generally board-shorts and baseball caps.

Sure you can go to the Sambadrome and see the feather headdresses and buttocks but you'll be doing it with 10,000 other people in 40 degrees heat (and no shade) and will pay a king's ransom (700 US dollars per person per night anyone?) for the privilege of a piece of concrete to stand on. When you're five foot and a fag end tall, like the missus, you're also not guaranteed you'll see over or around the obnoxious bloke who's jumping up and down in front of you either.

And would you believe you can pay more than a thousand US dollars to go to one of the balls! I'd run down Copacabana beach naked shouting 'Brazilians can't play football' before doing that.

I have to say that if the cost keeps going up and the spectacle isn't better coordinated and concentrated Salvador may well become Brazil's Carnival capital. Which might not be a bad thing.

We had to conclude that a) it's not the party it's billed as and whilst the main parade is a great spectacle you may come away from the whole carnival with a slight feeling of disappointment and, b) for the same price watching the jiggling girls and boys in tight pants you could rent a beachfront hotel room, with balcony, for the period of the whole event. And drink champagne every day.

So here's a tip, if you're going to Rio (and you should because it is a lovely place) spend your money on a really nice hotel at either Copacabana or Ipanema beach and spend your time seeing the sights and enjoying the beachfront bars and babes. If you go when the Carnival is on make sure you've brought a big wallet and as long as you're not expecting a party to end all parties or every girl to be a Bond girl you'll come away with some great memories and maybe not too bad a hangover.

What a view!

Sugar Loaf and Corcovado mountains have to be the two main highlights of our trip to Rio.

There are others such as the Santa Teresa district which was particularly lovely. It's got a famous and rather picturesque ancient viaduct at its centre and what makes it even more interesting is that there's a San Francisco-style tram line on the top. To see the trams go across with people hanging off the sides is quite a sight. There are also some wonderful old houses and narrow cobbled avenues hugging the hillsides. They even have one steeply stepped walk that disappears up a hill that's completely covered in colourful tiles. Add the louvre-shuttered-window bar area that used to be a red-light district and you have a place with some character.

The Maracanã stadium is a real slice of history for soccer fans too. Built for the 1950 World Cup it held

100,000 people. And for the final most of the crowd was Brazilian. All of whom were fully expecting their team to thrash Uruguay. They were somewhat disappointed. I bet you could have heard a pin drop that day.

There are also the lovely beaches of Copacabana and Ipanema which I mentioned earlier. If like me you don't want to fry go to Copacabana fort and take the view from under the trees at the local café on the water's edge. Very civilized.

But, back to the mountains as these really are the highlights.

The view from the cable car ride up Sugar Loaf Mountain and the subsequent view from the top are glorious. Same for Corcovado, where you'll first be looking up rather than down to take in the colossal art deco statue of Jesus – *Christ the Redeemer*. You're at a seriously high viewpoint over Rio up here which is brought home by the constant stream of helicopters hovering close overhead bringing the well heeled and time limited to see the famous statue. They then drop steeply back down to their helipads along the coast below. You can see the whole of the city, its beaches, the archipelago of islands just offshore and even the odd samba parade or two from here. Quite a photo.

Plan to spend a day getting to these two famous sights as everyone else wants to see them too. We hired a guide for the day and according to him there is no day of the year that it's not busy. Hiring a guide does however provide some respite from the crowds as they have an official pass that lets you breeze past the regular queues. When it's 40C and humid believe me the price of a guide is worth the convenience.

So there you have it. Rio de Janeiro. Worth a visit even if there's no party going on.

It's not the Amazon but could well be better

The Pantanal is the largest wetland in the world. It's a little like the Okavango Delta we visited in Botswana but without the hippos and elephants.

They've thoughtfully replaced those here with crocodiles.

Well, that's a little dramatic as the ones you'll see aren't the monstrous Nile or Salties that will make light work of you and your boat if you happen to stumble upon one in Africa or Australia. These ones are a more manageable two metres long and called Caymans.

They're everywhere and you can get up close and personal. Which is great for taking photos. They're also more afraid of you than you are of them. Which is also great for keeping your arms and legs whilst you're taking photos.

Our *pousada* had several caymans close to the

lodgings. As well as many more all over the neighbouring farmland. On arrival this is a little perturbing and even more so when the owner tells you to check in the pool before you jump in as there may be a cayman or two having a dip (only half jokingly). But it's hot out here, they're a little shy and they don't like to move much in the daytime, so you soon stop worrying.

I went walking one day and nearly stepped on one. I only noticed when he made a guttural noise to say 'Oi, watch it, big foot!'

It's the same with the capybaras. We'd seen these in the shop windows of Buenos Aires and Rio. They make a lovely pair of boots. In the flesh they smell a little bit more like a sewer than freshly polished leather and are somewhat hairier. And would you believe they're the largest of the rat family. Looks like a brown guinea pig the size of a sheep.

I was hoping we might see a cayman trying to catch one but no such luck.

The same was true of trying to see a jaguar. Apparently they like to eat caymans but as they do this at night it's a little like trying to catch Bill Clinton in flagrante with an intern. You know it's happening, you just don't know where.

In fact, trying to see rare and colourful wildlife in most of the world is tricky because they've mostly come to realize that man is not to be trusted. But in the Pantanal we have found a place that you really can see a lot of indigenous animals and birds without too much effort. We were here in the off season but still there is an explosion of life all around.

We nearly went to the deepest, darkest part of the Amazon further north but after researching it came to the conclusion we'd probably have more chance of seeing the animals we wanted to see in the Pantanal. We were right.

This area is also the home of beautifully colourful macaws, toucans, giant storks and howler monkeys. Not to mention a cacophony of frogs and snails. Yep, they've got giant snails that click. Very loudly. And crab-eating foxes. And frog-eating owls. Weird but true.

Horse trekking through the wetlands

I'm not a horsey sort of person. I do love horsepower though, when it's contained inside a V8 engine. When it neighs and is contained between my legs I'm not so keen. I've never ridden them as a young man and have only ever had two experiences of them up to this point. Both bad. Would you believe, I've spent more time on a camel. I once rode one for a few days across a Middle Eastern desert. Not the most comfortable mode of transport but a nice memory nonetheless.

It was also in the Middle East that my equine adventures happened. One was in Egypt on a donkey. I know that's not a horse but it's from the same family. You wouldn't believe how such a docile and apparently stubborn animal could move so fast. In the wrong direction.

It also gave me pause for thought on a mountain pass on the way into the Valley of the Kings when it seemed to have a death wish by walking perilously close to a very large vertical drop. I was pulling so hard on the reins for it to turn left, away from the edge, that I thought they'd snap. The reins strangling the damn beast would also have worked out but neither happened. I was ready to get off many times, but convinced myself I wasn't riding a lemming so shouldn't really expect it to commit suicide. I'm here writing this so obviously made it.

But the *coup de grâce* from my hooved foe was on the way back to the Nile. When passing through a small town it made a bolt for it. Everyone else was going straight ahead, and I was heading in the opposite direction (for no apparent reason) toward a local market at what seemed like dangerous speed. Yes, I know it was only a donkey but I tell you what, when you're about to run into a crowd and its little legs are going ten to the dozen (and your spine is being compressed several times a second by the short stabbing gait of the thing) everything becomes a blur. The locals were flailing their arms and shouting and finally the sheer number of people in front of me managed to stop it.

Thinking about it now, I can see the amusing side of what must have looked hilarious. At the time my arse was twitching like a rabbit's nostrils.

And then there was the horse I rode in the Dubai desert. Me and the missus had been assured that our rides were both very docile and I had to admit that hers looked like it was only a few days away from a trip to the glue factory but would you credit it, the old trooper was as randy as an eighteen-year-old boy after a gallon of Red Bull and several Viagra.

You guessed it. Mine of course was a female. Oh hilarity.

So you can probably imagine that I wasn't filled with great optimism about my Pantanal horse ride having these as my experience to date. But I'm not one to give up easily and anyway my two teenage nieces seem to be able to handle horses much bigger than the cute brown ones I'm now looking at, so ...

Entering the corral we're told by the gnarly old *Pantanero* (local cowboy) that they're really docile. Where have I heard that before! One of them seemed to be looking at me quite intently. Well actually, he wasn't so much looking as staring. I never saw him blink. I was hoping I would have had a female as they're known to be more gentle but on closer inspection I could see that this one was male. He'd had his nuts removed though so maybe he was docile after all. Although, if someone had removed my nuts I wouldn't be in the best of moods.

And he was still staring at me. God, I hope I didn't remind him of the guy with the knife, or pincers or whatever implement they used to turn him into a horsey eunuch.

I decided to go over and give him a pat to try and break the ice. He promptly broke wind. And then took a dump.

Getting on was easy enough though and when I'd had a quick refresher from the *Pantanero* on how to steer I found this horse handled really easily. A slight pull to the left and he went left. A slight pull to the right and he went right. A dig in the ribs from my heels and he speeded up and a pull back on the reins and bugger me if he didn't stop. Splendid.

I found out within half a kilometre though that he didn't like insects. Or dead twigs on the floor. Or water. Or his shadow. For what seemed like no reason at all to me he'd jump at the sight of any. To top it all, he seemed to be seriously flatulent. As the missus was plodding along behind she was complaining a bit. I reassured her it wasn't me but that didn't seem to change the expression on her face.

There were quite a few flies in the beautiful wetlands

we were wading waist deep (for the horse) through so I was advised to pull a leafy branch off the many saplings dotted around and swat them on the horse's neck and head. That would help calm him down.

Flagellating a flatulent horse. What is this place doing to me?!

It worked though and I have to say that if you find yourself out in the glorious natural expanses of the Pantanal go see it on horseback. We also hiked and canoed and used a truck a couple of times but the horse ride was a highlight for me. Amazingly.

Going Eco

Our lodgings were billed as an 'Eco lodge' on the web. This wasn't what attracted me to sign up though (it was the prospect of having some amazing wildlife on my doorstep) as I'm a little sceptical about such things. The word 'green' or 'eco' or 'environmentally blah blah blah' have become so universally abused it's almost certain the claim is a little hollow.

But it turned out it wasn't.

This area of Brazil is one of three ecosystems in the state of Mato Grosso. There's Amazon rainforest in the north of the state, savannah in the middle and the low-lying wetlands where we were. We're bordering Bolivia approximately 100 kilometres from anywhere with a shop or petrol station.

The only people out here are ranchers and a handful of tourists staying at the few private lodges and farms that take them in. But within this lovely landscape is an oasis of calm, cattle, caymans and eco friendliness.

The couple that own the *pousada* we're staying at

are well-travelled environmentally conscious types but not in a lentil-eating hasheesh pipe-smoking type of way. This much is obvious when we first meet and get talking. They are intelligent and have a well thought out plan. Their idea is an holistic approach to keeping the Pantanal pristine so they and everyone else who comes to live or visit enjoy it for generations to come.

A worthy pursuit indeed.

It turns out that Andre is also the pioneer of eco-tourism in Brazil. Since the early 90s he's been actively trying to get people to think about sustainability and giving at least as much as you take. Rather than keep talking he's put his money where his mouth is and is now leading by example.

A conservation project involving macaws, a sustainable tourism business and a working cattle farm are a passion for him and his lovely lady and you can feel this in every part of the *pousada*. They grow all their own fruit and vegetables and the beef couldn't be fresher, obviously. Water and waste is recycled and anything that's not is taken away from the Pantanal to be disposed of responsibly.

The macaws have been rescued from wildlife traffickers by local authorities and brought here to recuperate and then be released. They seem to like it though and hang around even after they've been set free. Wonderful for anyone who loves to see one of nature's most colourful creations. Plus you get to feel good because you know that your tourism dollars are going towards this and other conservation projects he's running.

He's kept the lodge rustically simple, but with flushing toilets, air-conditioning, a pool and wireless internet it's not exactly a hardship to be comfortable here. We loved it.

I did have one additional suggestion for them though. I'd seen an idea on the internet, apparently started in Brazil, that seemed like a good way to add to their eco credentials. It was for saving water.

A toilet uses between six and eight litres of water every time you flush it. That's a lot of potable water just to act as a means of removing urine eight times out of ten. It's hot out here and you go out on activities most days so are bound to get sweaty and need to take at least two showers a day. Why not save water and pee in the shower?!

Seemed to be a good pub point and got a laugh but I don't think he's about to start advertising just yet!

A Kit Kat moment

I mentioned that our lodge has a macaw conservation project. This is focused on the Hyacinth Macaw, which in turn gives the ranch its name. The Hyacinth is a gloriously blue-purple giant parrot with yellow-ringed eyes and a yellow flash across its cheeks. And they're frequently flying around close by. Absolutely wonderful to this sometimes birdwatcher. They've also got blue-and-yellow macaws and these are just as lovely if not quite so rare.

Getting a good photo of the Hyacinths is proving tricky though as the buggers seem to keep dealing me a Kit Kat moment.

I'll explain. In the not too distant past the Kit Kat brand ran an advertising campaign in the UK that had the tagline 'Have a break, have a Kit Kat'. One of the adverts was a photographer patiently waiting outside the giant panda enclosure at a zoo for the pandas to come out. He waited through sun, snow, wind and rain and then decided to take a break with his snack bar. As soon as he turned his back, the pandas came out. On skates. And proceeded to put on a show. Just as he was finishing and getting ready to sit at his camera again to get a shot they disappeared back indoors before he saw them.

Now, whilst I'm seeing the Hyacinth Macaws I'm having no luck getting a good photo. Or even a reasonable one. Hence the Kit Kat moment. I've had a couple of times when they've flown right by me. Just after I'd packed my camera away or was looking in the wrong direction at the wrong moment.

The best I've got so far was to stumble upon a couple in a tree and get a silhouetted photo or two in the fading daylight before they flew off.

In contrast I have some really good shots of blue-and-yellow macaws. They're such beautiful birds and seem to be happy to sit around while you snap away. All the locals keep telling me it's normally the same with the Hyacinths. I'm struggling to concur to date but have resolved to get geeky and sit around for a day waiting. Having already seen everything bar a jaguar (but I sort of knew in advance seeing one of those would be like seeing a leopard in Africa: damn difficult) I've decided this gorgeous bird warrants the time.

As the sun was dropping in the sky and *Pantaneros* were driving a cattle herd through waist-deep water, past caymans on the banks and miniature frogs chirping I had to admit defeat. Although the scene I was witnessing was something of a compensation. It was truly the sort of thing you'd see on a David Attenborough wildlife special.

I had of course seen my quarry and enjoyed that but was somewhat miffed I hadn't got a good photo.

But then on the last afternoon of the last day it happened.

One of the guides called me from my room as a pair had landed in a nearby tree. I jumped out of the shower and naked bar a towel ran camera in hand as quickly as my soaking wet feet would take me across a field. They were making a real racket perched about ten metres up in the branches. A little bit of slow repositioning on my part to get some light onto their beautifully coloured feathers and ... click.

Come to the Pantanal. You may have to get naked to see the rare stuff but you'll leave with a big smile on your face, I guarantee.

Pretty Polly's pretty difficult to catch on film!

North America

United States of America

America had often been discovered before Columbus, but it had always been hushed up. (Oscar Wilde)

The good old US of A. Home of the free and the loud. And Homer Simpson.

It all seems so familiar. And that's true whether you've been to the States before (like me) or you haven't (like the missus). You see at least a part of it on TV or in the news virtually every day of the year, seemingly whether you want to or not. The power of the media has well and truly been mastered over here. Goebbels would have been proud. Michael Jackson has been reputed to be more well known than Jesus Christ and who hasn't heard of Elvis, Madonna, Frank Sinatra and heaven forbid, Paris Hilton?

Most people would probably know the names of more Presidents from the US than from their own country, too. This is helped by the fact that in recent times, one was an actor, one was a Casanova and the last one was a lost cause with an ability to cock-up even the simplest actions.

And when you go to Washington DC you can see the Presidential monuments. They're pretty impressive for the famous chaps, including Washington, Jefferson and

Lincoln. I'd like to say the John F Kennedy Centre is too but from the outside it's not a classic. The Smithsonian is though. Reputed to be the largest museum in the world, it's a great place to learn about the States on a day like today when you're likely to get frostbite on your eyeballs. We also went to see the White House. It's not as big as it looks on the TV. But then again neither is Tom Cruise.

The rest of the capital couldn't have been more impressive though. A wonderful mix of modern and old architecture sitting side by side in a clean and well organized metropolis. The main government buildings are as imposing as anything you'll find in Europe. They're big.

And that is a word that of course is synonymous with most of our stereotypical views of this country. Big cars, big skyscrapers, big industry, big ideas, big people and Big Macs.

I'd also add to this, big portions.

Now, everyone loves the thought of value for money and the word value is one you hear a lot in the US. It's never price or cost it's always value. You see it all the time on the TV. There are whole channels dedicated to selling stuff it seems and they all talk about value.

And it's a supersized concept when it's something you can put in your mouth. The idea of less is more just doesn't apply. Unless you've had nothing to eat all day or have worms you're going to struggle to eat a full three-course meal here. Or even two-course. I'm not exaggerating. Me and the missus have rarely had more than the starters or one starter and one main course. To share. The food portions are huge.

Growing up in the UK the only time you'd eat as much as is offered up here daily, seemingly in every outlet, is at Christmas. Remember how full you'd feel after eating Christmas dinner? Imagine that every day. No wonder everyone here is either constantly jogging or at the other end of the scale, waddling around.

Laxative pills and gym equipment are advertised a lot in the States.

Even the seemingly sensible approach we've been taking usually results in food being left on our plates, and this brings me to the main point of this story.

President Obama is on the TV every day commenting on the need to help those who've lost their jobs as a result of the economic meltdown. Amazingly this is centred on food. Can you believe that?! Americans who need food. There's even a charity called 'Feeding America'.

Now in the restaurants and bars of the big cities you'd be hard pressed to spot the financial downturn. From what we can see everyone is having a good time and spending on cocktails, wine and steak. We've even struggled to find a table in a couple of places we wanted to eat in. But if you stay still long enough you'll see signs of the problem.

We loved our time in Key West and South Beach Miami. The drive down to the Keys is stunning (with a drive along some of the longest bridges in the world, that link the islands together) and when you get to the last island of Key West, the locals are friendly, the margaritas are flowing and the sunset parties happen every night. Hemingway would still be having a hoot in this most southerly point of the States if he hadn't shot himself.

Similarly the art deco architecture along Collins Avenue and Ocean Drive in SoBe are lovely. The fact that every other one has a bar and restaurant makes it one great place to spend your day. And your night.

Sit down on a sunny afternoon for a seafood salad and a mojito and listen to the live music and people partying in the street (Rio could learn a lesson!). But pretty soon you'll see the beggars. They're asking for your change so they can eat. Now I know that this happens everywhere in the world but it's not what you expect in the bastion of the free world where everyone has the opportunity of getting to the top no matter what level they started at (again, think Obama).

I've yet to visit a country where the locals are more attuned to selling themselves and as a consequence you never really know whether these people are in trouble or whether they are chancers. You feel good about giving if you know your money is going to help someone. You feel the opposite if a chancer is putting your cash towards his investment portfolio. So there's got to be a way to figure out the difference, in my book.

I have been to a country where I've seen a great personal approach to the poverty problem, ensuring you target the needy and avoid the chancers. I used to work with a guy in the Philippines who would take a very practical approach to teaching his two young sons about how lucky they are in life. They weren't rich but lived comfortably and he wanted his kids to know that their life doesn't come for free. He'd take them to the restaurant they wanted to go to, for example MacDonald's (okay, that's not a restaurant but it fits with the American theme), but wouldn't let them have everything they wanted. Instead he'd tell them that there was a certain amount of money available and for that they had to buy three meals. One each for them and one for someone else. That someone else would be a street kid.

I was with them one day when he did this and he then asked the eldest son, who was about six, to hand the extra meal to a street kid when they came over to ask for money. Which invariably they would.

Now, here's my idea. We sat and watched virtually everyone in Miami order a minimum of two courses. And promptly leave a large portion of it as there was just too much food. At the same time the homeless and hungry (and no doubt the chancers too) were coming past asking for money to buy food. Why not just give them the food that's about to be thrown away? You'll soon realize who the chancers are as they won't be hungry and will keep pushing for cash whilst the real poor and hungry will take up the offer.

Now look, I'm not suggesting you ask them to sit down or even to start eating your half-eaten Lobster Thermidor (and that's on the menu more frequently than a burger down here in Florida) but add a little intelligence to my point and there has to be a way to figure this one out.

I know for a fact that certain fast food restaurants have to throw away their pre-prepared food after it's been on the shelves for a certain period. Can't these products then be sent to a street kitchen for distribution to the hungry? Hell, I bet the kitchens would send a member of staff over to pack it up and take it away. Why would the restaurant do this? Well, their waste food disposal costs reduce for starters. And there's got to be a marketing angle surely.

I think there really is something in this and if someone who can do something is reading this then please feel free to get on with it. You have my full support.

I Heart NY

I've been coming here for years and love every time I land. Without doubt this is one of the most iconic, energetic and exciting cities on the planet. And it's all so familiar.

There have been so many movies and TV shows made here it's hard not to walk down a street and stumble on a famous sight. Home of De Niro, *Sex and the City* and of course Batman. And not to mention 'The King of Broadway', Nathan Lane (watch *The Producers* and tell me I'm wrong!). What's not to like? It's changed big time since *Saturday Night Fever* and *The Godfather* too. I'm not just talking flared jeans, big hair and moustaches either; the crime levels have dropped to the point that you just don't feel unsafe. Unless it's dark and you're in Harlem.

The streets are generally clean and the people nearly as friendly as those you'll find down on the beach in Florida.

The place assaults your senses at every turn. The smell of hotdogs and sugary snacks for the nose, the unmistakable sound of a cop car for the ears, massive skyscrapers for the eyes, a chill wind for your skin and coffee on every street block for your tongue.

Oh, and a naked cowboy in Times Square for your sense of humour.

Well he's got a pair of boots, a Stetson hat, a pair of Y-fronts and a guitar. And a smile, but that's about it. It's early March here and I'm wearing three layers and boots. It's freezing but this dude is smiling, singing and playing. Must have something to do with the long line of ladies queuing up to have a photo and a hug.

The missus has never been to the Big Apple so we're

off doing the touristy things (like checking out the cowboy) but to be honest I really don't mind as I love re-acquainting myself with this city and it's always a pleasure to take in the sights.

Working for a company based in North America historically meant I flew through a couple of times a year. On the way home I'd stop off either to see a friend in Manhattan or just to spend a day walking the Brooklyn Bridge, hopping on a water taxi to see Lady Liberty, taking in a Broadway show, having a coffee in Soho or walking around Central Park. Seeing the city from the top of one of the skyscrapers is a wonderful experience too. Try the Rockefeller as an alternative to the Empire State as the one thing you can't see from the top of the Empire State is the Empire State and what's a bird's-eye view of Manhattan without that in the frame?

I came here in 2001 and went up one of the twin towers. What a view you got of the East River and the famous Manhattan and Brooklyn bridges. And of course the iconic art deco skyscrapers of midtown. Who could have guessed that a few months later they'd be gone.

But you can't keep a place like this down and whilst you could never say that New York *is* the US it is a big influence on the way the rest of the country thinks and acts, in my view. It's also a big part of the world's perception.

And this brings me onto the Museum of Modern Art.

It was raining today so rather than walk the streets we headed to MoMA for a spot of culture and hopefully a few smiles. I love art but only the stuff that has an aesthetic beauty (in my eyes) or makes me smile.

MoMA has all of these things. Chagall's happy

goats, Dali's melting clocks, Warhol's soup and Magritte's clouds are always nice to see. So are Brancusi's and Koons' sculptures. This time they had a gallery showing Tim Burton's art too. Yep, that Tim Burton. When you look at his works you can see how from an early age he managed to imagine the delightful craziness of some of his most famous movies. It's all as mad as a bag of squirrels and I just love it.

And I love the fact that there's a whole floor dedicated to industrial design (think buildings and cars), household objects (think chairs, lights and juicers) and the like.

What I can't be doing with though are the types of 'art' that just seem like the emperor's new clothes. You know the story, the emperor was convinced by a scam artist that he was wearing a fantastic new outfit when in fact he was naked. Everyone around him was too polite, or more likely scared, to tell him so around he went as naked as a cowboy in Times Square (without the guitar).

I mean, how can a piece of two by four nailed to a wall be art? And what about a piece of wire shaped into a rectangle and leant against a wall? And my personal favourite, for the emperor's new clothes award, a perfectly blank canvas hung on the wall. How can this be of any interest to anyone?

It's all a load of Jackson Pollocks.

Surely this is just super-rich people buying into the next hyped trend because they've got nothing else to spend their money on.

But that then got me thinking about MoMA as a metaphor for New York City. The amazing skyscrapers that literally cover a large part of Manhattan island and give the city its unmistakable skyline were a pissing contest between the big boys. Those guys who drove the new economy of the newly rich US in the early 1900s wanting to see who could go the highest. Some of these are wonderful works of art such as the Chrysler and Woolworth buildings. Others are just concrete and glass and no one would miss them if they were replaced.

But their very existence makes you appreciate the good stuff. And there's a lot of that in the city, and the museum. And forget the idea that America has no culture. The architects of this city and the baby boomers that followed have shaped the popular culture of the planet for as long as I've been around.

So come and see it all. I challenge you not to smile at the sights and sounds and rave about your experience to friends when you go home. I love New York and I'm pretty convinced you will too.

Cowboys and Injuns

Rocks. Lots and lots of rocks. The Midwest is full of them. Mind you, they're a lot more interesting to look at than plains. And if you're in the rocky sections you won't be getting hit by a tornado either. Or so I thought.

Flying into Denver we were met by some wonderful blue skies and snow-topped mountains. And a tornado warning. What? I thought twisters only attacked the Bible-bashers east of here and the elderly in Florida.

Good job we're off to the Colorado Plateau pronto. Up here at over a mile high we're more likely to get hit by falling rocks than by the wind though. And what lovely rocks they are too. No really, I don't care if you're not that interested in what Mother Nature can sculpt; you'll be impressed with at least something this plateau has to offer. Arches and Natural Bridges National Parks have some spectacular, erm, arches and natural bridges. And the odd obelisk that looks like a giant penis. Really.

Even a spotty teenager who has reached the age when a grunt is the only sound used to communicate could raise a smile at that. And the area around Mexican Hat (great name) where Goosenecks (even better) and Monument Valley are will have you oohing and aahing. Or in the case of the missus saying 'Fuuuck' in a breathless hushed tone. Yes, they really are expletive impressive.

And does the Grand Canyon need an introduction?

And Lake Powell. Spend a day boating around the hundreds of miles of beautiful canyon coastline created by damming the Colorado River. You can get to the world's largest natural stone bridge from here too. Rainbow Bridge is something you shouldn't miss and at nearly the height of the Statue of Liberty you probably won't.

And my personal favourite, Bryce Canyon, where Mother Nature has seen fit to carve thousands of 25-metre-tall chess pieces out of pink, orange and cream sandstone. As far as the eye can see. The State of Utah and parts of the neighbouring states of Colorado and Arizona are turning out to be one hell of an outdoor playground. It's bloody fantastic. And it's Indian country too, so you can learn about the original inhabitants of the States before the white guys arrived.

Travelling further north to Wyoming and South Dakota you get to see where Custer got to stand, before being mowed down by the Sioux. The tribe have been building a massive sculpture into the Black Hill mountains for decades to celebrate this most famous of battles; hopefully it'll be as impressive as the Presidents' Memorial at Mount Rushmore just a few miles away when it's finished. It might take a while longer yet though as you can only see the face of the warrior Crazy Horse so far. He'll be sitting on a horse when it's finished so that's a hell of a lot of sculpting still to finish.

Obviously the cowboys are no longer at war with the Indians these days. The horses have generally been traded in for a truck and the fighting is limited to trying to pocket the tourist dollars. Oh, and both now wear cowboy hats.

And back in World War II they were wearing tin hats together. If you do a little reading at the various reservations we went to (like I did) you get to find out all sorts of things like this.

Yep, the Navajo fought in WWII as American soldiers. These are the guys who own the land that Monument Valley sits on. It's the place with giant red sandstone buttes and mesas that John Wayne and a bunch of other gun-toting cowboy movie stars used as a backdrop for their Wild West adventures. I guarantee you've seen a shot of it at sometime. But I digress.

The reason I'm selecting this particular tribe is that the Navajo are the famous WWII 'code talkers', the guys who were used by the American forces in the Pacific to relay messages across battlefields and from shore to ship. You see, their language is not based on any language that has a link to more widely used languages you hear today (whether it be Chinese, German, Swahili or Urdu) and is spoken by so relatively few people, none of whom lived outside of this region, it was a perfect way of keeping information secret from the Japanese. And it worked.

Mind you, if you were a Navajo code talker and got caught you were more likely to be shot by the Americans than the Japanese because they couldn't afford for the language to be deciphered. Possibly the last time the cowboys popped off a few Injuns.

The Injuns need fear the cowboys no more today though as they've got a new interest. Their attention is now focused on Mexicans streaming in to the US via Arizona.

Although, if you're in Vegas your attention may well

Yes I know it's childish but I bet you're smiling!

be on the Mexicans plying their trade on the street corners rather than the cowboys and Indians gambling inside the casinos.

Viva Las Vegas

How many movies have been made about this town? I'd wager that there are few on the planet who haven't heard of it and also dreamt of making a killing on the casino floor.

Started by the Mafia and perfected by corporate America this place is a testament to what you can do with lax laws and a puritan population gagging for sin.

The themed casino resorts are a textbook on what can be done with more money than taste, and a lot of cement and neon. Ultimately they're tacky but you can't help but be impressed upon first sight. Particularly if you're arriving shortly after the sun disappears over the horizon and the Strip's lavish lighting is providing an underscore of excitement to the blueberry-hued heavens.

A couple of them though have a real nice feel and are only let down by the clientele wearing board shorts and T-shirts. Come on America, dress up for a day or night out! Or just go to the less salubrious joints or the 'all you can eat buffet' so the rest of us don't have to see you.

But as I'm not a gambler, for me the best thing about Vegas is the shows. Quite the best *Phantom of the Opera* you're ever likely to see and if you're into *Cirque du Soleil* you'll be struggling to pick one from the veritable menu of options. But I can recommend *Zumanity*. Not only do you get to see some of the best acrobats and performers you're likely to find on the planet, most of them ain't wearing much. If you've ever wondered what those Olympic female gymnasts would look like after puberty, clad in nothing more than a G-string and a spot of eyeliner, then wonder no more. And if you're a girl there are a few six-packs strutting their stuff and if you're gay and couldn't get in to see Cher the singing will also make your night. It's headed up by a transvestite who looks like he's escaped from *The Rocky Horror Picture Show* and a French-Canadian 'audience fluffer' who's taken one too many Viagra and you'll be howling with appreciation for adult-only entertainment by the end. It's also the sort of Vegas happy ending the missus won't need to file for divorce after witnessing you enjoying either.

And that's why this show and some others like it are more fun to me than gambling. You win every time. And it's real entertainment unlike hitting a button on a slot machine over and over again or sitting at a card table or the roulette wheel with several other people who've had a personality by-pass. No really, have you been to a casino recently? No one talks to anyone else, the dealers have been lobotomized and there aren't any of the larger-than-life characters that populate the casinos in the movies. It's like being in a nightclub on nerds' night.

But surely we didn't come to Vegas without gambling at least a little, even knowing that the odds are stacked in the casino's favour? Well, we gambled on a top restaurant or two and had our wallets lightened significantly and the one-armed bandits managed to secure a five-dollar investment from the missus but that aside we generally stayed clear, preferring the shops, malls and café's. Being Singaporean and by default a world-class shopper, the missus was in heaven.

But isn't this defeating the point of coming to Vegas?

Well possibly but I don't think so. There are so many activities to do here you could spend your whole time never seeing a casino gaming room. Which is fine with me.

And there's free entertainment on the streets. You're constantly dodging Mexicans, seemingly freshly bused in from the border, selling 'girls to your room in 20 minutes'. Yep, prostitution is legal here. And in your face. And it's not just these guys with the hard sell. The sales approach from virtually everyone you come across is relentless. Whether it's timeshare condos, cocktails or cards everyone's got an angle. Wall Street could do with a few of these guys to get the economy going again.

Then there are the college jocks drooling over yards of ale and girls on hen nights who forgot to put on a complete outfit. Okay, the latter can be a good thing when they're wearing underwear and not falling over on their skyscraper heels. But none of this grates as I've been around the block a few times and can let it wash over me, enjoying it all as street theatre. And it's free!

You really don't see kids here and that's probably a good thing given the fact that there's absolutely nothing for them to do until they've got a credit card and some hormones raging. And you really wouldn't want them running the gauntlet of Mexican pimps and horny teens chugging cocktails as they saunter down the Strip.

But with this many shops, bars and fun things for adults to do we could and did survive our time in Vegas. Our hotel was on the Strip. It was funky and fun and I could see the Eiffel Tower from my window. We even had an in-house show starring rather a lot of Hugh Heffner's ex-Playboy Bunnies. And a few of their friends who pole-danced between the card tables to help you feel a lot better about losing this month's wages.

It'll make you smile just to experience such a crazy hedonistic place but probably won't win your heart. It didn't mine, but I did spot a few places to come back to with the boys!

Cars big as bars

The car is probably as synonymous with the States as the scooter is with Italy and long walls are with China. They didn't invent it but Mr Ford and his peers certainly productionized it and made it within reach of the average Joe. It's hard to see a house without two and hard to go anywhere without jumping into one. This place is built around it and no matter who you are and how much money you've got you're almost certain to have one. And if you haven't got one you probably live in Manhattan, or under a bridge. In a box.

So we're obviously using this most wondrous contraption to get us around. Which is good as by now you've probably figured out I love them. And we've used several to travel some forty thousand kilometres around various chunks of the world on this trip.

I also think that America is so intrinsically linked to the car that coming to the States and not talking about it a little would be amiss. They invented the drive-in diner, which morphed into the drive-thru and if you've been to Las Vegas, like we have, then you may have also spotted a drive-thru wedding chapel. Gives a whole new meaning to the phrase 'a quickie'. And of course none of these inventions could, or would, exist without the car.

We've covered a large chunk of America from the east coast to the west and would not easily have reached a lot of the wonderful places we've visited without the use of a few.

My preference is a sports car as you can take the top off, they better connect you to the road and they're easily the best looking cars. Really. Just take one five-year-old, put several cars in front of him and I guarantee he or she will pick the sports car as the coolest car in a nanosecond.

So what's the States got that's worth a go in?

I've often thought that the Corvette Stingray was a wonderful metaphor for America. It's loud, brash and fast. It's also a Marmite thing. You either love it or hate it. It was born in a time America was king of the hill and has hardly changed since. Massive engine, two seats and an interior by Tupperware.

Well, I figured it was probably a good idea to have a go in one. Whether you love it or hate it it probably has more bang for your buck than most of the supercar competition. Amazingly you can hire one for a few days at a fraction of the cost of a European alternative too. So I did.

We got called early in our room on our second day in Los Angeles and headed downstairs ready for a couple of days in our new ride. The valet brought it out of the garage and I have to say that I couldn't keep a smile off my face. In the plastic this thing is very handsome. It was bright yellow and a convertible. And boy would it look completely out of place in the UK, or anywhere else actually. Unless you were a porn star or a wrestler. But here on the streets of America it looked just so.

And by God it shifted.

I face-achingly enjoyed taking my first blast up Pacific Coast Highway 1 in this quite stunning convertible, but what took it to a whole other level was handing the keys to the missus.

A petite (and if I do say so myself), gorgeous Singaporean filly flooring an uncommonly sexy American muscle car whilst letting out a sound you'd pay good money to hear on a chat line. Oh lordy!!!! The start of a new auto game, or is it just me?

But generally we couldn't get away with the fun stuff because we've got a fair bit of luggage and that means we needed space. Not hooning around in a dragster saves a few bucks too.

So, something more middle of the road then. And this seems easy in the land that invented the concept that you can't have too much choice. Even with the recent financial meltdown and several car brands disappearing it's easy to pick up a very good choice of rental wheels for a reasonable price. The competition is fierce and like a good consumer I took full advantage. What amazed me most though was the size of the cars. The average saloon has to be a good foot wider than the models I've normally driven in Europe and Asia. And a fair bit longer too. And that's just what they call 'intermediate'.

America frequently gets slated on the world stage for driving gas-guzzling SUVs and trucks. And here in the Midwest and the Rocky Mountains I would defy you to spot anything other than these V8 trucks. Now to me, 4x4s are for the Dakar Rally, farmers and rappers. But out here it appears everyone including the maid has one. I didn't even use a proper 4x4 in South America where it would have been easy to justify, so driving along the highways of the States doesn't seem to warrant their use but here we are surrounded by them. I've never liked these massive machines and see little reason for their existence. They're heavy, bulky, have poor performance and efficiency and are downright ugly. Generally, their drivers are also completely oblivious to other road users as they lumber around the streets looking for things to squash.

In these times of belt tightening and the search for smarter ways to use the earth's energy resources you've got to ask yourself what sort of a prat would still be driving such a thing?

I was still asking that question as I stepped up into the driving seat of mine.

This thing was damn near as big as the lake it's named after. I've got a mate in Tokyo with a smaller apartment than this monster. It's like driving your living room. And whilst that makes it comfortable it does have the handling characteristics of a blancmange.

Hypocrite I hear you say. How could you defend driving such a thing. Well, fair comment but I do have a defence of sorts. Would you believe they had no smaller vehicles available? Really. I'd have had to wait half a day for the car I'd actually rented to return. And they gave me this one for the same rate.

Aw come on, give me a break. I normally drive cars with much smaller engines. And the whole point of my writing is to convey something of the real country visited. How can you do this with the States, a car-centric country, without driving one of their most popular products?

Plus, after driving it for a few weeks now I've come to the conclusion that it has two redeeming features. And I wouldn't be able to impart this consumer feedback without having driven one, now would I?

Whilst it has the aerodynamic properties of Pavarotti

holding a fish tank the high-up driving position gives you a wonderful view of the countryside which is a new experience for me. You can see over walls and fences and most shrubbery and trees too. When you're in Yellowstone National Park and there are bison walking past you and the odd grizzly bear (really) being this far off the ground in a yank tank is a pretty nice place to be.

It's also safe when there aren't any animals around. Yeah yeah yeah, I know what you're thinking. Of course it's safe. That much metal hitting something is going to flatten the something and maybe result in you getting a light belly wobble in the process. That's not what I'm getting at though. Inadvertently this behemoth may have cracked the age-old problem of how to get motorists to stick to the speed limit. With comedy suspension and the stopping ability of an over-excited puppy your survival instinct constantly tells you to take it easy.

We found many roads with 75-mile-an-hour speed limits which was nice , and debunked the myth that the blanket speed limit in the States is 55. Driving a full-size SUV at much more than 75 miles per hour is something I'd recommend you don't do. Unless you want to become a candidate for the Darwin Awards. You know, those awards that are given out to persons who are stupid enough to remove themselves from the gene pool. Like flying a kite in a thunderstorm or using a metal-handled knife to get your toast out of the toaster while it's still toasting.

So there you go. If I'm given the choice I'd prefer the dragster over the SUV. It's a lot more fun if somewhat impractical. As opposed to being practical and no fun. Both are best on the open road away from the city.

Both are an American experience worth having and you'll most likely survive going fast in one and slow in the other.

You may not survive the ridicule when you finally get back home though.

The car only looks small because Bonneville Salt Flats is so damn big.

The jewel in the crown

Did you know that America invented the idea of the national park? Yellowstone was its first in 1872 and we've just been there. We've driven up from Salt Lake City where we stopped off to see how fast the rental would go on the Bonneville Salt Flats. Not that fast as it turned out as the salt was still a little squishy from rain but fun nonetheless.

The park has only just opened for the season now the snows are receding, albeit it's snowing when we arrive. It's stopped the following morning though and the snow is providing a wonderful winter backdrop with the now blue skies.

Yellowstone sits on the world's largest super volcano. It didn't explode while we were there as I'm writing this, and you're reading it, but apparently it's due sometime soon. Thankfully, soon in geological terms is probably long after we're all pushing up daisies. You do get to see plenty of geysers exploding though, including probably the world's most famous, 'Old Faithful'. And then there are the natural hot pools and sulphur lakes. All wonderful to see in a bright but chilly climate as the hot steam rises up into the air.

This scene was made even more enchanting by the presence of bison and elk. The bison made it for me. They're imposing but somehow very cute with their furry coats and fluffy faces and an adorable little goatee beard. There were even a few recently born calves. All very picturesque.

I love bisons.

Not sure I could eat a whole one though. Luckily for me they serve them up in the local eateries in more manageable portions.

A bison burger is a thing of beauty and I must recommend you try one. I'd steer clear of the rocky mountain oysters though. I'm generally open to try most foods but a bison's gonads is where I draw the line. Or any genitalia for that matter.

We even saw a wild grizzly bear! Oh, how happy I was. And this is exactly the same state of nirvana I've been in travelling through quite the most comprehensive set of geological areas any one country on the planet could offer. The fact that the US has decided to turn these areas into national parks means that you should be able to enjoy them for centuries to come just as I'm experiencing them now. I've already talked about the parks on and around the Colorado Plateau. We also went to the Everglades in Florida, the Volcanoes on Hawaii, the Redwoods in California and to my mind the best of the best, Yosemite.

This place has a valley with waterfalls cascading from giant granite cliffs on both sides into a valley floor, carved by glaciers, of lush green meadows with a smattering of brightly coloured flowers, pools that reflect the granite cliffs above and beautiful groves of deciduous and evergreen trees. After a sunny day walking around by the river and taking in the flora and fauna and glory of nature at its fertile best, go in the

Bison make for an interesting alternative to SUV's on the road.

late afternoon to Glacier Point and then Tunnel View. If there was an Eden it would surely have looked something like this.

We've been to twelve national parks on this trip through the US and there are another forty-six you can visit. All in all they cover an extraordinary range of plants and animals and geology. It's no surprise then that *National Geographic* has spent a lot of time documenting them.

So, there it is. My vote for one of America's best ideas. Right up there with them deciding to speak English.

Feel the love

I've decided that my favourite US city is San Francisco.

Yes I know that New York is more vertical and LA has more movie stars and Miami has better beach bars and Seattle has better coffee and Denver's got skiing and Washington's got better memorials and everywhere's got less fog but San Francisco just feels nicer.

This loving feeling isn't the feeling you get when you land at the airport and drive through a fairly industrial part of the greater bay area, but as soon as you get to the city and pass age-old street trams, the Bay Bridge, people on segways trundling down the road and experience the golden Californian light in the afternoon you just feel warm and at home.

It's somehow peaceful and vibrant at the same time. Home of famous inebriated anti-establishment writers and poets, the summer of love and protest in decades past, you can still get a sense that should you fancy burning your bra or rollerblading naked down the famous hill streets of this multi-racial city then you should just go ahead and do it.

We didn't see either but we did spend some time walking around the various neighbourhoods of beautiful Victorian houses, taking a coffee or something stronger in some of the street café's (Vesuvios being the most famous on account of Jack Kerouac's patronage), visiting Alcatraz (it's worth it for the bay view alone) and riding on the cable car.

The cable car is such good fun. You get to hang off the side as it trundles up and down the famous hill districts. The view's fantastic and the experience something you'd think would have been banned as too dangerous in such a litigious society. In India we saw people hanging off the sides of buses and trains. You can do the same thing with the open-sided cable car here. You just stand on a footplate, hold tight onto a handle and breathe in every time a car or another cable car comes the other way. Just like they did in the old days. Wonderful.

San Francisco is also the home of arguably the most famous bridge in the world. The Golden Gate is a wonderful sight and if you pick the right car (a convertible) and the right time (late afternoon so that the sun is over the Pacific Ocean) you'll have an eyeful of its bright red splendour. Driving over to Sausalito you head up a mountain road to the daddy of all vantage points to see this man-made wonder in all its glory. If you're lucky, like we were, the sun will be shining, the famous fog will be rolling in from the Pacific, but won't yet be hitting land or the bridge, and there will be just a slight breeze. You feel that close to the bridge that you could almost touch it. You can see the cars below and the boats below them. And through the suspension structure you can view the city and clearly see the Pyramid, Coit Tower, Alcatraz and the Bay Bridge in the distance. It's magical and my vote for one of the best free views on the planet.

When you've had an eyeful and got your breath back, head down the hill into Sausalito, park up and find a waterfront café for an early dinner. Watching the sun go down and the lights coming on in the city across the bay is just one of those things you should spend an evening doing.

I know I'm starting to sound like I've joined the bay area tourism board but this place has got under my skin. And would you believe there's more?

Napa and Sonoma's vineyards are forty-five minutes up the road and if we're talking about roads there is of course the famous Pacific Coast Highway 1. Keep hold of the convertible you hired the day before and head south to Big Sur. You won't be disappointed. You might get a little sunburnt but the extra sensory experience an open top gives on such a glorious road is worth it. The ribbon of tarmac kisses the beach and rolling surf on most of the trip. And just after Carmel you'll see some of the most beautiful and dramatic coastline California has to offer. You'll be smiling all the way and maybe be feeling the same love this city was famous for all those decades ago.

You may even forget that it's sitting on a major earthquake zone.

Aloha Hawaii!

When I was a kid Hawaii was probably the place that was as far removed from the British Midlands, where I grew up, as it was possible to get. We had concrete, grey skies and miners and they had surf, sun and girls in grass skirts. Oh how I wanted to go.

And to make it even better they had a cool guy in a red Ferrari with a big moustache and two very animated eyebrows who always seemed to be getting the girls, with or without grass skirts. I'm humming the theme tune to *Magnum P.I.* as I type this. I was never keen on growing a moustache and I didn't want to be chased by two bloody great Dobermans on a regular basis but I did fancy the car and the girls. Even if it meant I had to wear one of those flowery Hawaiian shirts.

Well, it's taken me forty years to make it but finally I'm here.

This is essentially our final stop in the US and our final beach holiday of the whole trip. We've split our time between Oahu, Kauai and Big Island. I use the local term for the latter as it's actually called Hawaii but that gets confusing as the world knows the complete set of islands as Hawaii. So Big Island it is.

All are volcanic with Kauai being the oldest and Big Island the youngest. Kauai is by far the prettiest with a blanket of greenery draped across the island that makes it feel very tropical. The green is vivid with a capital 'V'. When you marry that with volcanic mountains several thousand feet high whose walls plunge near vertically into the turquoise waters of the Pacific you've got one of the world's most impressive coastlines. We took a helicopter to get a good look at the eye-wateringly beautiful Na Pali coast and I'm here to tell you it was the best value sightseeing flight I've ever been on. No it wasn't cheap but by God it was spectacular.

We'd managed to snag the front seats next to the pilot so had a wonderful view. This guy had been used by the *Jurassic Park* film crew to take them to some very inaccessible parts of the island and I could see why. I've been on several helicopters historically but none were this smooth. He'd got a soundtrack running to accompany the flight that went from *Mission Impossible* and James Bond theme tunes to the *Jurassic Park* theme tune as we headed up and only just over the top of the Manawaiopuna Falls and into a windy, steep-sided river canyon, before pitching up and out and across to the Waimea Canyon. You go from tropical rainforest to mini Grand Canyon in the blink of an eye and before you know it you're heading back to the coast and the ocean. And this is where you get to see the mind-numbing beauty of what this island has to offer.

Flying close enough to a razor-edged ridge that I felt the need to pick my feet up you pass over its apex and the green-cloaked volcanic rock just drops away. As the helicopter banked right pitching me downwards I had an unobstructed view of such vivid blues, whites, reds, browns and greens as my eyes flitted from ocean to beach to land. I didn't know where to take a picture first. Really. I've seen some glorious natural sights in my life and also on this trip but the Na Pali coast takes some beating. Nowhere to my knowledge does this array of primary colours exist on a coastline that also has crazy green volcanic mountains with waterfalls dropping two thousand feet, from cloud forests above, into vertical ribbed gullies that you could hide several Empire State buildings in.

We flew in and out of a couple which is a weird sensation as you get close enough that all you can see below and above and to the sides is foliage draping sheer volcanic cliffs. Several had waterfalls and the spray from the falls drenches the helicopter. Pivoting and coming back out just takes you back to the riot of colour and form of the coast. All to the soundtrack of 'I can see clearly now the rain has gone'. Ha ha!!

I didn't want it to end. I'm still buzzing now we're on Big Island and about to take another helicopter flight. But this one is very different. This time it's to see one of the most active volcanoes in the world. Kilauea.

Walking to the helicopter two things crossed my mind. Firstly it had no doors. And secondly someone's grandmother was sitting in the pilot's seat. It seemed we were about to fly over lava fields and a sulphur spewing volcanic crater with Betty White! Sure she apparently had many decades of flight experience but her feet only just reached the flight pedals and who knew if Old Father Time was going to play a part when we were up there. Too late, we're off.

With no doors you can really feel the elements. A light shower we pass through on route feels like sand blasting on my elbow when it strays out of the cockpit. And when we fly low over the lava fields you can very definitely feel the heat. The lava wasn't exploding out of vents today. It was more like oozing. This gave a very unusual silver sheen to its surface as it cooled slowly. You could very definitely see the red-hot lava pushing slowly along the surface on the leading edge of the silver sheen. Quite a sight.

Only one mile from this most primeval of natural events was a lone house. And would you believe it's still inhabited. Jack Thompson is the King Canute of the lava world. His is the last house to be spared the burning inferno on his doorstep. From our helicopter you can see the streets that have been cut off by past lava flows and the burnt remains of a few dwellings. Amazingly, he's on a plot that is lush and green, with a great view of the ocean, and slightly raised so that the lava so far has gone around him on all sides. So far is the past twenty-odd years by the way. Everything has to be flown in by helicopter, including his guests as he rents out a room or two. Look up Jack's Lava House on the net. Makes for a very different holiday experience.

After Betty got us back home safely we drove the car to an area a couple of miles away from Jack's place to see what it looks like from the ground. It's forbidding. Black lava from historical explosions twisted and curled into savagely beautiful art that whilst impressive to behold wouldn't inspire the thought in my head, 'I'd like to live here'. But that's exactly what's happening as can be evidenced from several houses cropping up on the lava fields.

Mind you, there is a rather nice sea view.

Hawaii's a geographical gem nestled in the middle of the Pacific and it was definitely worth a visit. It might have been a good idea if I'd turned up a couple of decades ago though. The hotels we stayed at, like most here it seems, were right out of the new brutalist era, which probably was good-looking in 1980 (although I doubt it) but somewhat knocks the edge off the overall tropical feel to the islands thirty years later. Particularly when they're dealing up a rather package-holiday experience to boot.

But they were on beaches of rolling surf with giant manta rays gliding through the unpolluted turquoise waters so that helped somewhat. So did the seafood, which was fresh, and together with the very colourful drinks was served up with a laid-back casualness you can only really get in the Pacific Islands.

But, the main geological attractions aside I left with a tinge of disappointment. Yes, there are some great local villages, particularly on the north beaches of Kauai. And yes all the elements of a good island holiday are there but they somehow don't add up to the type of stunning holiday experience you can get these days in many locations in South East Asia, the Caribbean and the Indian Ocean. And the type of paradise Hawaii is billed as and the one I was hoping to see.

Magnum was the man of the moment when I was a kid but his re-runs are not quite cutting it anymore. Yes, they're still enjoyable in a certain way but not as good as the current crop of cops and robbers shows. It's a classic but, like the islands, in need of a makeover.

Do go and see the sea life, the volcanoes and the Na Pali coast but when you have, go in search of something a little more chic now moustaches are no longer the height of fashion.

England and America are two countries separated by the same language' (George Bernard Shaw)

We've spent more time in the States than in any other country we've visited. You might think this was a waste of time because surely after a few weeks the sugary food, loud locals, incessant advertising and soulless strip malls would have necessitated the need for a sharp exit, but you'd be wrong. Sure, if you frequent fast food outlets, sit in front of the TV and go to the discount shopping centres you'll collide headlong with many an ugly American stereotype. But select your cities carefully and after you've seen the sights, partaken of their buzzing bars and chic restaurants and socialized with the very friendly locals a little, get out into the wild west and you'll be rewarded with memories that will be right up there with the best the rest of the world can throw up.

Now, if they could just get rid of the guns ...

(and a little bit of) Canada

The North American Rockies are one of the most impressive wildernesses we've seen. So rather than stop in Montana and Wyoming we decided to keep going north to Canada to see some more.

This isn't a country that's new to me but Alberta is a state that is. We've arrived after the ski season and the winter Olympics. But that's okay as we wanted to miss the crowds.

It's still a little snowy and the scenery in Banff, Lake Louise and Jasper is stunning as a result. The sun's shining, the skies are blue and there aren't many people around. Canada's not the most populous of nations and out here in the west that holds true even more so. The backdrop all the way along our route is the Rocky Mountains range. It's magnificent.

This route from Calgary to Jasper has recently been voted the most stunning scenic drive in the world (according to the local tourist rag). I'm sure there are a few contenders around the Alps in Europe and I know there are a couple in New Zealand and Patagonia but it's not difficult to see why it's been voted. The road weaves along the bottom of a glacial valley with massive granite mountains on both sides sprinkled liberally with snow. There are many glaciers up here that you can just park your car and go and have a walk on.

The evergreen trees in the valley form a beautiful carpet of life between the mountains and the river that flows along by the road. It's frequently churning white water but in the calmer parts it's a milky turquoise thanks to billions of suspended particles washed down from the glaciers. Every so often it flows into and through a lake. Some are frozen over and others are partially thawed revealing a mirror image of the mountains above.

Why am I telling you all of this? Well apart from the fact it's worth writing down to bolster my memory for years to come (but I've a feeling this image will last a long time anyway) it's probably the image of Canada that you all feel familiar with. And I'm here to tell you that the contents are just as described on the box. All served up with lashings of maple syrup of course. Well, at least in Alberta and British Columbia as these are the only bits we're travelling through.

It's clean and fresh and just like one of those pictures on a box of chocolates from a skiing holiday. There are elk, mountain goats and marmots walking around and the locals couldn't be friendlier either.

All the food is just so, the supermarkets stock seemingly everything and a lot of it fresh produce from Canada. You'll love the seafood, fish and meat. Unless you live on a farm and carve a chunk off the beast or your dad's a fisherman it isn't going to taste fresher than this. They even make their own wine. And before you say anything, it's rather good.

We holed up for a few days in Lake Louise and then

Jasper, first in a small hotel that used to be a hunting lodge and still felt like a log cabin and latterly in the basement of someone's house. Unusual choices maybe but we'd just had enough of identikit hotels and motels for a while.

Both places have fantastic alpine scenery. The walk along the edge of Lake Louise to Victoria Glacier was a particular highlight. This is an incredibly picturesque pocket of mountains and when the sun is glistening off the snow and the thaw is creating small avalanches and ever-growing waterfalls you really don't care that the lake's frozen and you can't see the legendary turquoise waters.

I can see why so many Brits made their way over here to live. It's all very nice and just so. And when we had spent a few days in Vancouver (where they were celebrating Victoria Day in honour of Queen Victoria, which is more than us Brits do) on the Pacific coast we also found it can be rather wet. So it's just like the UK then, except with bigger hills, more snow and bears.

And it's the latter that most people would really want to see on a trip to Canada.

We saw a grizzly bear in the wild in Yellowstone, Wyoming. What a wonderful and rare sight. Prior to seeing it we also went to see a few in a wildlife park in the same place. It's definitely not the same as seeing a wild one but it does guarantee you can say you've seen one and as the park has gone to the trouble to try and treat the bears as though they're in the wild (for example, they make them forage for food) it gives you a great opportunity to view their habits. Anyway, the point is that additional to a couple of Yellowstone Grizzlies they also had a couple of Canadian Grizzlies. The latter were easily twice the size of the US version.

Seeing one of these in the wild in Canada is something the locals try and warn you against attempting. They are apex predators with a nose that can sniff out food from miles away. Sure they look all cuddly and fluffy but having seen one up really close in that wildlife park I'd rather not see one on a hiking trail. Oh yeah, they're also about the only animal on the planet that sees man as 'on the menu'.

You're more likely to bump into a black bear though. And we saw quite a few of those in the wild. They're a much more manageable size and are less likely to eat you. Mind you, I'm not sure getting too close is a good idea either. But the problem with these is that they like to come to see you. In town!

We spent a few days in Whistler north of Vancouver. It had just been one of the host venues for the Winter Olympics but was now populated with mountain-bike riders as the snow was disappearing. It used to be called Alta Lake but the marmots that live in the mountains around here whistle and captured the popular imagination. So the name got changed. Now when you consider that Canada has a history of coming up with some crazy names one shouldn't be surprised that a place got named after a musical rodent.

The US had some wonderfully named places. Sundance, Deadwood and Spearfish (and a creek called Crazy Woman) were some of my favourites. But Canada is in a different league. They start at this level of weirdness and then take it to a whole new ball game. Yellowknife, Moose Jaw and Beavermouth anyone? And then they really get into gear with my absolute favourite name of any place on earth: Head-Smashed-in Buffalo Jump. Huh?! Marijuana is somewhat tolerated out here in the west and you've got to think that the locals were smoking something when they came up with that one.

But back to the bears. We had a sleep in today and got awoken by a gun shot. Made me jump I can tell you. Particularly when it was followed by another that seemed to go off right outside our window. Pulling back the curtains and stepping onto the balcony I noticed through sleepy eyes that there was a crowd standing across the street looking in my general direction. I probably should have put some clothes on but they were there already so I doubt they were staring at me.

A wisp of a smoke trail shot up from below me into the three trees that stood between the hotel and the road, followed by a loud bang. I jumped at the sound and so did the tree right in front of me.

And then our eyes met. There was a black bear clinging to the tree trunk no more than ten metres away. Five storeys up. What a beautiful animal and what a fantastic encounter. I got some wonderful close-up photos and a good twenty minutes of wildlife theatre as the rangers tried to get the bear out of the tree and out of town and the bear was trying to stay put.

It seems a little cruel when you see the tactics used but I do understand why the rangers were trying to scare it. Associating humans with loud noises and a generally unpleasant experience will maybe avoid a few bear attacks in the future. Or at the very least stop them from breaking into cars and raiding trash cans.

But seeing these wonderful animals is an experience you come to Canada for so go search it out. You won't find it too difficult to see one if my experience is anything to go by. Unless you turn up when they're hibernating.

That said you really do need to take a few precautions. Walking around with a roast chicken in your pocket isn't a good idea and neither is going hiking on your own. If you're a Billy No-mates travelling on your lonesome then how about chatting up a few members of the opposite sex to take with you on your search for Yogi and Boo-Boo? You never know, you may get to see more than one type of bare!

You can also go to an outdoor clothing store and buy a bear bell so that you don't accidentally surprise one and they have time to move away before you arrive. Or maybe they hear the sound and it just tells them where lunch is! Do let me know which it is if you take this option as, of the people I spoke to, the jury still seems to be out.

Further north they've got polar bears. We didn't make it that far but at least one grizzly did. He humped a polar and created a new sub-species called a pizzly bear. Really, go look it up. I tell you what though, you've got to be some testosterone-charged fur ball to mount a polar bear!

Nature really rules up here and unlike the US where you feel man has tamed the beasts and largely got them holed up in national parks it feels the other way around in Canada. The wilds are just so big and the people (outside of the cities) so few that it's not difficult to feel a little small and insignificant. So much of the country is completely inaccessible for most of the year and probably not that accessible for the rest of it either. Everyone is basically living along the US border. That's not because they want to hop across but because the wilds are keeping them down there.

I heard a joke in Vancouver from a friend we'd met up with for a beer and a long-overdue catch up: Canada is bigger than the US and it's on top. If we were in prison the US would be our bitch.

Well from what I can see, with the massive land mass of largely uninhabited snowfields, tundra and mountains that make up the vast majority of the country, Canada is most definitely on top of the Canadians too. But I think you'll agree, sometimes it's nice to be on the bottom ...

Canada is nice. The place is nice, the people are nice and the overall experience is nice. They have some magnificent national parks and wonderful clean air. They've got one of the best backyards in the world, as the British Columbians would say.

So when it comes to land size, bear size and ice hockey the Canuks seem to be the daddy. But it's the overall quiet calmness to the place and the people that impressed me. The sort of calmness that comes from knowing you're getting it right.

Japan

Japan

A learning experience

Famous for video games featuring an Italian plumber, comics with sexy schoolgirl anime heroines, crazy game shows designed to humiliate and of course raw fish, perched on top of a smidgen of rice, Japan is our last stop on this wonderful sojourn around the world.

I don't know anyone who has visited and come away with a bad report so it should be good. And we've got friends here so that should ensure a good few nights out enjoying sake and sushi and a helping hand with the local language. The missus is especially looking forward to it; however, I suspect that may largely be related to shopping.

But here's the thing. We've been here for a few days now and, well, it's all a little bit quiet and normal. We've visited some of the world's most impressive sights and cities and seen some of the world's most spectacular wildlife and events on this trip around the world and after a little time in Japan I'm struggling to come up with a decent story befitting this journey and my sense of humour. I'm even struggling to come up with a suitable adjective to describe the place, hence my use of the rather non-descriptive 'normal'.

We haven't seen what I'd class as a world-famous building, even though they've got one hell of a lot of UNESCO world heritage sites. And don't say 'Tokyo Tower'. If you've seen the Eiffel Tower it's fair to say you're going to be somewhat underwhelmed by the Japanese effort.

They've got the world's longest suspension bridge but it's grey and not half as nice as the red one in San Francisco.

There's a very nice giant sitting Buddha statue but the one on Lantau Island, Hong Kong is bigger and in a nicer place.

And if you're into oriental palaces the ones in Beijing and Tibet are more grandiose and ornate.

It's the same story with the temples. They're all very nice but there's no wow factor as with, say, Angkor Wat in Siem Riep. Or if you need a North East Asia comparison, the Temple of Heaven in Beijing.

There aren't even any impressive animals here.

And the most famous event I can think of is two fat men wrestling each other in a heavy duty G-string.

Surely I'm missing something?

Well, yes.

It took me a while but I'm beginning to get it.

What you get in Japan is restraint and attention to detail.

Nothing's shouty and very little is done to excess.

It could be that the buildings aren't particularly impressive because Japan's been in the economic doldrums for more than a decade or it could be that they don't see the point in building elaborate erections to the sky just to show off. It may also have something to do with earthquakes. All 1000 plus of them each year.

And if you look at the buildings from ancient times you'd have to say that whilst there's a dour 'form fits function' simplicity to them this actually is very easy on the eye if you sit down and look at them for a while. Same goes for the gardens of manicured trees, stones and raked gravel. They may be old but (zen) style never goes out of fashion and good design has obviously stood the test of time.

Also, everything's clean. The Japanese clearly take pride in their surroundings and themselves as can be seen by the fact that there is no litter. And that seems to be achieved without the aid of public dustbins as I'm buggered if I've been able to find any when I wanted to get rid of a tissue or an empty drinks bottle.

Everything is done with care, patience and professionalism. I would evidence the efficiency even the most menial of tasks are seemingly completed with. I mean, have you ever seen a baggage handler load bags onto an airport bus without throwing or huffing? Most I've seen usually also do this randomly and with no particular urgency. Even more ask you to do it yourself. Usually by default of ignoring you. In Japan it's a well-worked procedure that the guys doing the job regulate with frequent checks of their watches to make sure the bus will leave on time. Then you're welcomed aboard with a greeting and a smile. I bet you haven't experienced that in too many places.

I live in a country where serving people is considered a necessary evil by a large portion of the locals and my homeland is even more famous for service with a sneer. In Japan it comes across as more of an honour. And the best bit, no one wants a tip! I frequently tried to give maids and bell boys a tip for cleaning up after us and lugging our (by now very heavy souvenir-laden) bags around and to a one they politely refused.

This even happened in Kyoto where, after exploring the leafy lanes, cobbled alleyways and Shinto shrines of the old capital we bumped into a couple of geisha girls. Yep, they've still got ladies who go through the training and rituals over many years to earn this title and wear probably the most famous face of Japan. To see these young ladies with quite the most glorious costumes just walking down a street with modern society all around is really something special. And, unlike everywhere else in the world we've been, they're happy to have a picture taken with you without taking your cash.

This trait is something you find a lot of in Japan. People are willing to do things without any thought for compensation in return. Twice, we've been lost in the sprawling metropolis of Tokyo and twice the Japanese person we've asked for directions has taken us to the destination we wanted to go to.

Taken us!

In one case this was in the opposite direction to which she was going and about a ten-minute walk. Again, know anywhere else this would happen?

And then there's public transport.

In a lot of countries this is frequented by the poorer end of society as they don't generally have a cheap alternative. In Japan, everyone uses it because it's clean and efficient. It's not particularly cheap but probably all the better for it.

Take the trains. The Shinkansen service, or bullet train, is probably the rail system that most foreigners would know of. We used this several times as it connects all the major cities and also some interesting places like Hakone and Kamakura. You can see Mount Fuji from the former (unless you go on a rainy and cloudy day, like we did) and several famous Shinto shrines and a big Buddha statue at the latter.

On this trip around the planet we've taken a few train journeys but these were by far the easiest, fastest and cleanest. And, joy of joys, you're not allowed to let your phone ring or talk loudly as 'it will disturb the neighbours'. It's the same thing in restaurants. And woe betide you if you've got an errant child running amok. All it took was an elder lady to glare at the mother and one child we saw was whisked outside for a telling off for no doubt inconveniencing the rest of the restaurant's clientele.

So it may not have impressive sights or other touristy things but by virtue of care and attention they do even the simple things well which makes it a very nice place to spend some time.

Now there's a novel idea most could learn from.

Much better than ripped jeans and T-shirts.

The weird and the whimsical

But it's not all peace and quiet.

We found out later that day that you can dress up in a hired Japanese outfit and walk the streets just like the geisha and samurai of the past. We didn't as the heat of the day was starting to make us wilt but a few did. Generally they wore yukata which is a lightweight version of the geisha outfit for the girl and a cotton full-length bathrobe with a thick belt for the boy, the ladies' being bright and colourful and the men's in more manly stripes or geometric prints.

Returning to Tokyo, we realized that dressing up in such outfits is the thin end of the wedge when it comes to the Japanese showing individuality, and maybe letting their hair down a little, too. I say letting their hair down as you really don't see this much in the Japanese way of life. Everyone's so respectful of others and polite in public.

Yes, in my working life, I've spent many an evening with a Japanese businessman who after being given plenty of sake and a karaoke microphone will transform from the epitome of Japanese reserve into a party animal but usually that's only in the confines of a soundproof room and not in public.

You really need to spend some time in Tokyo like we have to see what I'm getting at. In this sprawling metropolis of a city where some thirteen million people live in each other's laps it's probably not surprising that there has to be release from the rigours of work and the neighbours and dressing up seems to be one of them.

The Brits love to put on fancy dress assuming there's alcohol and an event but the Japanese are very happy to do this with neither. Particularly young ladies which, for a red-blooded male, is a very pleasant sight.

Think French maids, anime characters, gothic princesses, sexy ghosts (with white contact lenses) and probably the most iconic soft porn image of this land, the sailor inspired schoolgirl outfit. Although very often I think these females are actually schoolgirls! And they like the look enough to still be wearing them in the evening and during the weekends.

Kawaii is the word for cute in Japanese and kawaii rules in Japan. Dressing up to make yourself more cute would therefore be a natural progression I guess. I'm not sure where sex fantasy makes it into this theory but you only have to walk into a general store in an area like Roppongi or Shibuya and you'll find a whole floor dedicated to kinky outfits, leather underwear, masks and sex toys. There was a whole section for vibrators and dildos which was strangely right next to the deodorant. Everything from candy-coloured baubles to some-thing that looked like a truncheon with balls. Note I said a general store and not a sex shop in a red-light district!

We had a great few hours with a couple of friends messing around with outfits covering everything from a sexy geisha to a sumo wrestler to a naughty nurse to Sailor Moon. And no one bats an eyelid. Least of all the check-out girl who seems genuinely happy you've found something that will put a smile on your face.

Later that day we went to a themed restaurant. The theme being a dungeon.

Yep, it was underground and yep they had handcuffs and yep the waitresses had quite the most fetching short wardens' outfits on you could imagine and yep you were locked in a cell with iron bars. Oh, and half-way through dessert the ghosts and ghouls come

The dark side's looking more interesting every minute!

a-knocking and a-rattling. And yes the female ones were more sexy and cute than scary. Ha ha.

And it's not as though this is a one-off experience. Go to Shinjuku or Shibuya or Harajuku or Roppongi Hills and you'll find everything from shops selling used female underwear (really) to love hotels with rooms by the hour (a quickie anyone?) to café's where the all- female staff (wearing French maid outfits, of course) tell you how handsome, clever and wonderful you are (well obviously) to bars that have bars and nightclubs that have 'Benny Hill' moments and everyone runs around with their pants down. So I'm told ...

For such a reserved and polite people they sure know how to get it on in as many ways as you could imagine. And you know what, it's an absolute hoot. They seem to have perfected the art of sexy without seedy.

Now maybe this has something to do with the fact that they're all Japanese and so everyone has the same sensibilities and mindset. Or possibly madness. In the nicest possible way of course.

I know that's like saying that the people who live in Britain are all British but what I mean is they're all ethnically Japanese. In Britain they're not all original white islanders by any stretch of the imagination. In Japan you just get ethnic Japanese. I know that it's not the only country in the world like that but it's certainly the only island nation with a first-world economy that immediately springs to mind.

And indications are they'd like to keep it that way. There's probably more chance of them developing humanoid robots to take up jobs vacated by their famously ageing population than changing their immigration policy. Actually, I think they are already.

But at least the very Japanese-ness of the place will be preserved for all to scratch their heads at and smile.

It's the food, stupid!

I said at the start of this that there was nothing that gives the wow factor for the tourist in Japan but I purposely missed out one thing that does. The food.

This is really saying something when you consider that I live in Singapore where good food is considered a birthright by the locals, but it's true. Japanese food is rightfully world famous as a result.

There are so many different types too and like everything in Japan you find someone specializing in each. Whether you want teppanyaki, yakitori, sashimi, sushi, tempura or noodles it's easy to find. The same applies to different meats or fish.

I'd steer clear of the wasabi and octopus ice cream though. As a rule I find dessert is best left to the French and Italians.

Having local and *gaijin* friends to help out meant we got to experience some lovely local restaurants that weren't touristy. One had only fifteen stools, all along a bar separating the customer from the chefs. You had to bow under one of those low banners you find at the doorway of many traditional Japanese restaurants to get in, and when you did there wasn't room to swing a cat but the food was very delicious and gave you a really authentic experience of eating in Japan. It was just like you'd imagine it was going to be like before you actually got here. These places need to be sought out though as they seemed to be relatively few and far between. But they're really worth it.

Another was much larger but just as atmospheric. Quentin Tarantino went to this restaurant in Roppongi Hills district and liked the feeling and design of the place so much he used the layout and concept for a key scene in his *Kill Bill* movie. You know the one. Where O-Ren Ishii and her band of sword-wielding henchmen got sliced and diced by a Bruce Lee-inspired yellow-costume clad Uma Thurman. All to the cheerful beats of the 5, 6, 7, 8's. Couldn't help whistling along as we arrived. There weren't any Yakuza around but it did seem to be the haunt of all of the foreigners in the city.

That didn't detract from the experience though as the place really did make you think of the movie and the food was yummy.

And our favourite – a fish and wine restaurant that would have been at home in the famous Tsukiji fish market, which was where we'd started earlier that day. And what an early start. The tuna auction kicks off at 4.30am. You can then wander around the wholesale market and see all of the fish being packed and shipped. You can even try some for your breakfast.

We didn't as we were waiting to enjoy the day's catch at dinner time, tuna being the main sashimi item we wanted to enjoy. Japan is famous for its love of this fish so we weren't about to miss the opportunity. But this is just one of the myriad of seafood choices available. However, I was drawing the line at the uglier options and most definitely was not about to eat fugu (pufferfish). If not properly prepared it might well kill you.

Now look, I know I've been shark diving, bungy jumping, canyon swinging, mountain hiking, glacier climbing and big-game tracking with nothing more than a stick but I'm buggered if I'm going to shake off my mortal coil at the hands of a poisonous fish. Yes I also know that I've eaten some weird and wonderful fare on this trip but I draw the line at this. Animals shouldn't be able to kill you when they're dead. It's just wrong.

But the fish and wine restaurant we were being taken to that night was just right. It was one of those places that you'd never find on your own and you probably wouldn't find in a guide book. It was down an alley and wouldn't receive a second glance from someone who might just glimpse the large white lantern outside and several stacks of polystyrene fish containers (which we'd seen thousands of at the fish market during the morning). It was structured from plywood, had no shop front and most of the staff were wearing wellies. Yet it was packed the two times we went, with everyone from finely dressed young socialites to office workers to retirees. And this wasn't the weekend either.

The wine referred to in the restaurant's very functional name (Fish and Wine Restaurant) is rice wine which comes chilled or warm and in rather a large bottle. It was summer so we went for the chilled version. The missus and I like sake so it wasn't long before we'd downed a couple of glasses. In the meantime our friend had ordered the food and as the order was largely raw fish it didn't take long to arrive.

Sushi and sashimi is now as easy to get as a steak and fries in virtually any country. We've been eating really good sushi from New Zealand to America on this round-the-world trip. And I don't just mean in the cities. We even managed to find a really good one in the Andean Lake District. So expectations of this meal, in the land of its invention, were sky high.

And boy was it good. Fish as fresh as this doesn't really have any smell to it, except freshness itself. When dipped into wasabi horseradish and soy sauce it's just divine and melts in the mouth. Washed down with good sake, and even better company, a meal like this is hard to beat.

It's just different

Now, after all that food nature's going to take its course sooner or later and that's when you'll discover another area of Japanese life that's had some care and attention lavished on it.

The toilets here are something to behold. The Japanese are renowned for hi-tech but the toilet isn't the place you'd immediately think of finding it. It's like sitting in Captain Kirk's chair on the starship *Enterprise*, once you've got over the initial reluctance to park your bare arse on something that's plugged into a wall socket that is. These things have more buttons and settings than a microwave.

Thankfully it doesn't make food but if you want your ass warmed or cooled or sprayed or fanned it can do that. And the spraying bit makes sense at least. I mean, if you wash your hands after going to the loo wouldn't it be a good idea to wash the part of your body that's actually taking a crap? Mind you, I'd double check the water pressure setting before launch.

Thomas Crapper would have been proud. Although if he was on a high-speed train he might have a different view. Because here, you'll only find a couple of foot plates and a porcelain hole. Now, I don't know about you but I've always avoided squat toilets for fear of my trousers dragging through something or even worse my losing my balance and all of me dragging through something. There's a game show here called *Endurance* and this is exactly the sort of feat they'd have you perform to try and ensure your embarrassment and everyone else's amusement. To put one on a train that's moving forward at high speed, and in several other directions at the same time, seems like someone's having a laugh.

But what would I know. We haven't been here nearly long enough to figure out this place but I don't think that really matters. The ultimate feeling you have after visiting is that it's different, but you're not entirely sure how or in some cases why.

On the surface, Japan appears to be an eminently cultured and sensible place. Everyone's polite, everything is clean and efficient and there's a nice blend between old style and modernity. But scratch the surface and you find someone's let aunt Flo' out of the asylum without a chaperone.

Karaoke, anime, cosplay, near-naked sport, iconic porn, a bizarre game called Pachinko and food to literally die for.

There's nothing in Japan that we've seen that really makes you go wow (except the girls' costumes and the food) but everything is nice and comfortable. There's a local saying I was told about that likens it to a lukewarm bath. Not too hot and not too cold. And I've got at least one *gaijin* friend who doesn't want to get out just yet.

Epilogue

A year passes pretty quickly when you're busy.

Whether that's busy with work or family or learning or travelling it doesn't seem to matter. Time flies.

Busy isn't a bad thing from my experience though. Just as long as it's something you're busy enjoying. For me it's always been travel and the last year has not diminished that love one bit. It's actually reaffirmed my desire to continue to soak up as much of the flora, fauna, geology and human culture of this planet in the years ahead that I can.

Was it heaven all the time? Well no, not entirely, as even the best laid plans can go wrong. Like the day we found out the Brazilian visa rules for my wife had changed since we'd set off from Singapore, and we didn't know. We were offloaded at the air gate when the officials figured out, rather late in the process, that the relevant stamp wasn't in her passport. It's a fairly stressful experience I can tell you. We had to get over our emotions and think quickly to figure out a way of getting the necessary visa, find a hotel for at least one extra night and organize a new flight as soon as possible. Not achieving this would have meant missing a much anticipated Christmas at Iguazu Falls. But we figured it out and enjoyed our Christmas as planned.

And of course the time we were in the middle of the desert in Rajasthan, close to the Pakistan border, and I got food poisoning from a local vegetarian dish the guide had recommended as 'the meat wasn't so fresh'. The missus had, on reflection, quite sensibly decided to eat nothing. Me being a polite Englishman thought I'd better try something as they'd specially prepared it for us. Big mistake. Later I found out that the toilet didn't work without leaking. And there was no air-conditioning in the tent we were staying in. It was 40 degrees Celsius. And we had a twelve-hour car journey the next day. Again, we coped and it's a funny story now.

And of course we had the odd argument or two. Know any married couple that doesn't? Considering we were in each other's pockets 24/7/365 these were remarkably few and far between though.

I guess this just goes to prove the old adage that you don't get anything worth having without some effort and a little discomfort every now and then.

But it was so worth it. The whole trip was joyous, educational and life reaffirming in so many ways. We came back a year older but feeling ten years younger and many years wiser.

I said at the start of this book that you should spend more than just an evening, weekend or annual holiday doing exactly what it is in life that you enjoy. If, like me, that's travelling then I hope my experience will prove in some small way to be a catalyst that sees you become a time-out traveller too.

About the author

Darryl Sailor grew up in rural Staffordshire which is a small county on a small island in the North Atlantic. And whilst a nice place for horses and grass it wasn't the best place for a young man with itchy feet.

After an ill-advised summer holiday or two in his teens, with 'the boys', where the only thing discovered was a hangover, he quickly changed tack and went off trekking, climbing, driving, diving and sailing large parts of the world in his spare time to see what was out there.

Twenty years later he's still at it.
And now living on an even smaller island.
In the South China Sea.

Lightning Source UK Ltd.
Milton Keynes UK
08 December 2010

164084UK00001B/29/P